Wow! This is

Allergy Free

and Sugarfree

Artwork by Mary Yoder

First Printing June 2001
Second Printing September 2007

© June 2001 Apple View Publications

ISBN 0-9711105-1-4

For more copies contact:
Apple View Publications
4495 Cutter Road
Apple Creek, OH 44606-9641

2673 TR 421
Sugarcreek, OH 44681

Carlisle Printing
OF WALNUT CREEK Ltd.

Acknowledgments

We are indebted to our families and wish to thank each one for their support and help in various ways to bring about the completion of our second cookbook, "WOW! This is Allergy Free".

Thank you, Diane, Darla, and Dorisa for all the hours spent in the kitchen in altering and perfecting these recipes until they were just right. Danae, thank you for assisting in whatever way you could.

To our husbands — Thank you, Jake and Harold, for believing in us, and encouraging us on with this project.

Our thanks to you, Diane, for the fine work with the graphics, and also for your assistance with proofreading.

Thank you, Brian, for your patience and excellent work in proofreading the document.

Gratefully,
Deborah Steiner and Mary Yoder

Introduction

There have been many requests for more helps with allergy problems and also for stevia as a sweetener, which has brought about the need for this second cookbook.

In this book we will be telling you what has worked, and is working, for us. We are all different. If one thing doesn't work for you, try different things until you find what does work.

We have attempted to help you to find what your intolerances and allergies are by helping you to keep a food diary, and eliminating for a time the foods you suspect are causing a problem for you. The section with daily menus is designed to help you plan your meals around the Four -Day Rotation Diet.

Our aim is to give you healthy, nutritious recipes that are nourishing and will with time help your body to heal itself. We do not usually become ill overnight, and we will also need to give our bodies time to heal. In our society it is not always easy to stick with a healthy diet, but it is well worth the extra effort it takes to do so.

I have had allergy problems for many years. About 5 years ago I had the Ig G ELISA blood test done, which also tests for hidden delayed reactions. If you would like more information on the Ig G ELISA blood test call IMMUNO LABORATORIES at 1-800-231-9197. Along with the blood tests, the doctor also introduced me to the Four-Day Rotation Diet, which I have adhered to since. I am now able to enjoy many foods I could not tolerate five years ago. Some foods are no longer a problem, while others my body can handle as long as I eat them in moderation and don't eat them more often than every four days. However, there are still some foods I can't tolerate even on the rotation diet.

I have had low blood sugar for over 25 years. I was told to eat lots of protein and not many carbohydrates. I ate lots of meat - often a quarter pound several times a day. It kept me going, but I slowly kept getting sicker and sicker.

Since I am on the rotation diet, my blood sugar has leveled out to the point that I don't feel the need to eat between meals, nor at bedtime. We eat chicken and fish only occasionally - not even once a week - and beef mostly just in social settings. We get our protein from nuts, seeds, whole grains, beans, and lentils.

Since on this diet, I no longer have weight gain problems, which I have had since childhood.

We do not use dairy products, except occasionally for social reasons; however, on the rare occasions when we do, we no longer have reactions to them. My husband has had sinus problems ever since I've known him. Since he has eliminated dairy products, his sinus condition has greatly improved.

You will find that our recipes sometimes list various options, such as "1 cup apple juice or water". The apple juice is preferable since it is listed first, but the water has also been tried and works if you are not able to use the apple juice. Also, when there are several options on a recipe that are designated for a specific day, such as *(day 2)* on the rotation diet, the first item listed is the one that goes with that day, such as "1 cup spelt or kamut flour". Spelt goes with *(day 2)*, but kamut will also work.

I hope these recipes and helps will be as helpful to you as they have been to us.

Mary Yoder

Table of Contents

(continued)

Table of Contents (Continued)

-- Charts --

WEIGHTS AND MEASURES

3 teaspoons = 1 tablespoon

12 teaspoons = $1/4$ cup

4 tablespoons = $1/4$ cup

$5^1/3$ tablespoons = $1/3$ cup

8 tablespoons = ½ cup

$10^2/3$ tablespoons = $2/3$ cup

12 tablespoons = $3/4$ cup

14 tablespoons = $7/8$ cup

16 tablespoons = 1 cup

2 tablespoons = 1 liquid ounce

1 cup = ½ pint

2 cups = 1 pint

4 cups = 1 quart

4 quarts = 1 gallon

8 quarts = 1 peck

4 pecks = 1 bushel

16 ounces = 1 pound

ABBREVIATIONS

Tbsp. = tablespoon
tsp. = teaspoon
oz. = ounce
lb. = pound
qt. = quart
w/ = with

COOKED FOOD MEASUREMENTS

1 cup uncooked rice = 3 cups cooked

$1/3$ cup uncooked lentils = 1 cup cooked

SUBSTITUTIONS

1 Tbsp. cornstarch = 2 Tbsp. flour or
1½ Tbsp. quick cooking tapioca

1 tsp. baking powder = $1/4$ tsp. baking soda +
½ tsp. cream of tartar

1 oz. unsweetened baking chocolate =
3 Tbsp. carob powder + 2 Tbsp. butter or
fruit juice conc.

STEVIA CONVERSION CHART

Sugar	Stevia Herb (green)	Liquid stevia
1 cup	1 tsp.	1 tsp.
1 Tbsp.	$1/8$ tsp.	6 drops
1 tsp.	pinch	2 drops

Fruit Source & Barley Malt	Stevia Herb (green)	Liquid stevia
$1/4$ cup	1 tsp.	1 tsp.

Note: Stevia Extract (white) varies in sweetness.
Try one-half or less of the amount you would use of the Stevia Herb (green).

Four-Day Rotation Diet
Day 1

Beverages: cashew milk
soy milk
grape juice

Fruit: banana
cantaloupe
honeydew
grape
mango
pear
raisins

**Green
Vegetables:** alfalfa sprouts
cucumber
dandelion
endive
garlic
green beans
green pepper
onion
parsley
salsify

**Yellow
Vegetables:** carrot
parsnip
pumpkin
tomato
winter squash
yellow pepper

**Cereal,
Grain,
& Flour:** arrowroot starch or powder
amaranth
flax
oat
rye
soy

Seasonings: basil
cayenne
dill
oregano
sage
savory

Meats: Cornish hen
goose
venison

Fish: mackerel
sardines

**Nuts
& Seeds:** cashews
pumpkin seeds
soynuts

Legumes: black turtle beans
lima beans
northern beans
navy beans
pinto beans
soybeans

Four-Day Rotation Diet
Day 2

Beverages:
rosehip tea
apple juice
orange juice
pineapple juice
almond milk

Fruit:
apple
avocado
cherry
cranberry
date
lemon
orange
pineapple
tangerine

Green Vegetables:
asparagus
bok choy
broccoli
kale
mushroom
okra
spinach

Yellow Vegetables:
cauliflower
rhubarb
sweet potato

Cereal, Grain, & Flour:
buckwheat
spelt
teff

Seasonings:
black pepper
cinnamon
cloves
nutmeg
turmeric

Meats:
duck
lamb
turkey

Fish:
cod
haddock
halibut
perch
pollock

Nuts & Seeds:
almond
pecan
sesame
sunflower seed
walnut

Legumes:

Four-Day Rotation Diet
Day 3

Beverages: mint tea
papaya juice

Cereal, Grains, & Flour: kamut
quinoa
tapioca

Fruit: blueberry
fig
kiwi
papaya
watermelon

Seasonings: caraway
celery seed
coriander
curry powder
rosemary
tarragon
thyme

Green Vegetables: beet greens
celery
chard
chives
leeks
lettuce
zucchini

Meats: chicken

Fish: roughy
sole
tuna
whitefish

Yellow Vegetables: beet
eggplant
summer squash
potato
yam
water chestnut

Nuts & Seeds: chestnut
macadamia
peanut
pine nut

Legumes: adzuki beans
black-eyed peas
carob
garbanzo beans
kidney beans
lentils
mung beans
peas
snow peas
split peas

Four-Day Rotation Diet
Day 4

Beverages:
apricot juice
Brazil nut milk
grapefruit juice
prune juice
rice milk
coconut milk

Cereal, Grain, & Flour:
barley
cornmeal
millet
rice
whole wheat

Fruit:
apricot
blackberry
coconut
grapefruit
peach
plum
prune
raspberry
strawberry

Seasonings:
cumin
ginger
marjoram
mustard seed
saffron

Meats:
beef
veal

Fish:
salmon
trout

Green Vegetables:
brussels sprouts
cabbage
collards
escarole
mustard greens
turnip greens

Nuts & Seeds:
Brazil nuts
butternuts
carob
filberts
hickory nuts

Legumes:

Yellow Vegetables:
corn
kohlrabi
turnips

Daily Menus
for
Four-Day Rotation Diet

Before shopping for groceries, check upcoming menus for recipes which may contain ingredients you don't normally stock in your pantry.

Always check the day before to see if any preparation is required ahead of time. For example, grape nuts for breakfast, bread, dairy free cheese, etc.

If a food on the menu is unappealing to you or not available, substitute with another food or recipe for that day. Be patient, your taste buds will adjust and actually learn to appreciate foods you initially thought were not appealing.

If you prefer your larger meal at noon, switch the lunch and dinner menu.

Freeze leftovers for snacks or quick meals. Be sure to mark which day it is to be used.

Lettuce is one food that seldom causes reactions. Many people are able to enjoy it every day with no problems. Have a variety of lettuce so you can rotate between different varieties.

It is a good idea to occasionally switch to different brands to avoid reactions. After a period of time, a person may start reacting to olive oil. By switching to another brand, the problem can sometimes be eliminated.

Day 1

Breakfast: Cooked Amaranth p.3
Banana

Lunch: Pepper Venison Sandwich p.80
Carrot sticks

Dinner: Spaghetti Squash Casserole p.52
Thinly sliced cucumbers w/
    Vinegar & Oil Dressing
                      p.103
Apple Cake p.109

Day 3

Breakfast: Cooked Quinoa Cereal p.3
    w/ blueberries

Lunch: Blackeye Pea Soup p.66
Kamut Crackers p.153
Kiwi

Dinner: Chicken Potato Casserole p.34
Sauteed Eggplant p.84
Tossed Salad p.100
Carob Chip Bars p.119

Day 2

Breakfast: Buckwheat Pancakes p.5
Apple

Lunch: Creamed Turkey Sandwich p.79
w/ Sourdough Spelt Bread p.25
Spinach Apple Salad p.99

Dinner: Parsley Breaded Fish p.59
Sauteed Spinach p.88
Broccoli Cauliflower Salad p.95
Apple Pie p.137

Day 4

Breakfast: Blackberry Muffins p.14
Grapefruit

Lunch: Salmon Puffs p.60
Green Leafy Salad *
Millet Rice Cake p.110
    w/ rice milk

Dinner: Cabbage Rolls p.57
Corn Bread p.19
Strawberries

*Lettuce is one food that seldom causes reactions. You may be able to use lettuce every day. We suggest you rotate between varieties of lettuce.

Day 1

Breakfast: Grape nuts p.4
Pear

Lunch: Basil Green Bean Soup p.73
Rye Crackers p.152
Cantaloupe / Honeydew

Dinner: Golden Chicken p.57
Green Beans
Oven Fried Winter Squash p.89
Amaranth Carrot Cake p.108

Day 2

Breakfast: Cooked Kasha p.3
w/ apple juice or almond milk
Orange

Lunch: Turkey Noodle Soup p.77
Broccoli Spinach Salad p.95
Diane's Cinnamon Swirl Bread
p.19

Dinner: Fish Filets p.58
w/ Sourdough Spelt Bread p.25
Orange Asparagus p.83
Cherries
Pecan Sandies p.123

Day 3

Breakfast: Blueberry Tea Cake p.113
Papaya Juice

Lunch: Lentils p.38
Chive Potatoes p.86
Tossed Salad p.100

Dinner: Oven French Fries p.87
All-in-One Salad p.95
Apple Dumplings p.128

Day 4

Breakfast: Rice Pancakes p.5
w/ Blackberry topping
(use Blueberry Topping
recipe) p.6

Lunch: Barley Cabbage Soup p.65
Blackberry Muffins p.14

Dinner: Oven Fried Fish p.59
Cabbage Slaw p.96
Millet Rice Shortbread p.20
w/ rice milk & berries

Day 1

Breakfast:	Cooked Steel Cut Oats p.3
	Pear
Lunch:	Cream of Bean Soup p.70
	Rye Crackers p.152
	Cucumber Salad p.96
Dinner:	Crock Pot Vegetable Soup p.72
	Green Pepper Strips
	Melon Medley p.131

Day 3

Breakfast:	Cooked Cracked Kamut p.3
	w/ blueberries
Lunch:	Golden Baked Potato p.85
	Lentil Burgers p.61
	Celery filled w/ Peanut Butter
Dinner:	Baked Chicken p.55
	Quinoa Dressing p.42
	Potato Salad p.98
	Zucchini Bread p.21

Day 2

Breakfast:	Grape nuts p.4
	Blackberries
Lunch:	Quick Drop Biscuits p.13
	w/ Turkey Gravy p.34
	Sweet Potato Almond Salad p.99
Dinner:	Spinach Turkey Salad p.99
	Steamed Cauliflower p.90
	Soft Pretzels p.154
	Apple Crisp p.127

Day 4

Breakfast:	Cooked Millet Cereal p.3
	Peach
Lunch:	Cabbage Soup p.67
	Barley Crackers p.152
	Raspberries
Dinner:	Rice w/Salmon Gravy p.34
	Green Leafy Salad*
	Peach Pie p.139
	w/ Coconut Crust p.140

*Lettuce is one food that seldom causes reactions. You may be able to use lettuce every day.
We suggest you rotate between varieties of lettuce.

Day 1

Breakfast: Cooked Oatmeal Cereal p.3
Banana

Lunch: Salmon Puffs
(use Mackerel) p.60
Carrot Sticks
Pumpkin Walnut Cookies p.123

Dinner: Spaghetti Squash
Casserole p.52
4 Bean Salad p.97
Banana Cake p.109

Day 3

Breakfast: Cooked Quinoa Cereal p.3
Blueberries

Lunch: All-in-One Salad p.95
Baked Potato Chips p.85
Quinoa Carob Cake p.112

Dinner: Chicken Stuffed Zucchini p.49
Golden Baked Potatoes p.85
Celery Sticks
Watermelon

Day 2

Breakfast: Buckwheat Pancakes p.5
Fresh Pineapple

Lunch: Kale Soup p.74
Spelt Thins p.153
Darla's Spinach Sandwich p.78

Dinner: Fish Filets p.58
Sweet & Sour Broccoli-
Cauliflower Salad p.95
Pecan Muffins p.16
Baked Apples p.128

Day 4

Breakfast: Fried Millet Mush p.7
Grapefruit

Lunch: Barley Cabbage Soup p.65
Millet Rice Cake p.110
w/Strawberries

Dinner: Cabbage Rice Casserole p.33
Green Leafy Salad*
Shortbread Cookies p.124

*Lettuce is one food that seldom causes reactions. You may be able to use lettuce every day.
We suggest you rotate between varieties of lettuce.

Day 1

Breakfast: Cooked Amaranth p.3
Pear

Lunch: Bean Patties p.55
Rye Bread p.27
Grean Leafy Salad*

Dinner: Golden Chicken p.57
Cucumber Salad p.96
Pumpkin Pie p.139

Day 2

Breakfast: Whole Grain Pancakes p.6
Avacado

Lunch: Turkey Noodle Soup p.77
Broccoli Spinach Salad p.95
Apple Pull Apart Bread p.22

Dinner: Dorisa's Pigs in a Blanket p.80
Steamed Broc. & Caul. p.90
Fresh Fruit Salad p.93
Baked Donuts p.18

Day 3

Breakfast: Blueberry Muffins p.15
Papaya Juice

Lunch: Baked Fish p.58
w/ Kamut Sourdough
Bread p.26
Quinoa Pea Soup p.75
Celery Sticks

Dinner: Skillet Tuna Potato
Casserole p.44
Tossed Salad p.100
Kamut Fig Bars p.120

Day 4

Breakfast: Rolled Barley Cereal p.3
Blackberries

Lunch: Salmon Puffs p.60
Steamed Cauliflower p.90
Corn Bread p.19

Dinner: Cabbage Rolls p.57
Green Leafy Salad*
Barley Cookies p.121
Plums

*Lettuce is one food that seldom causes reactions. You may be able to use lettuce every day. We suggest you rotate between varieties of lettuce.

Day 1

Breakfast: Granola p.4
      w/ soy milk, cashew
     milk, or grape juice
  Banana

Lunch: Bean Soup p.66
  Rye Crackers p.152
  Cantaloupe

Dinner: Pizza p.41
  Carrot Sticks

Day 2

Breakfast: Buckwheat Grits p.3
     w/ Apple Juice

Lunch: Creamed Turkey Sandwich p.79
  Sweet Potato
     Almond Salad p.99
  Rhubarb Crunch p.134

Dinner: Dressing-Noodle Casserole
      p.40
  Steamed Cauliflower p.90
  Cranberry Apple Pie p.137

Day 3

Breakfast: Blueberry Pancakes p.6
     w/Blueberry Pancake
     Topping p.6

Lunch: Eggplant Patties p.84
  Finger Lickin' Good Potatoes
     p.86
  Tuna Salad p.100

Dinner: Easy Chicken Casserole
     p.34
  Tossed Salad p.100
  Carob Cupcakes p.114
  Kiwi or Watermelon

Day 4

Breakfast: Cream of Rice Cereal p.3
  Strawberries

Lunch: Cabbage Soup p.67
  Barley Crackers p.152
  Berry Crisp p.129

Dinner: Rice w/Salmon Gravy p.34
  Quick Drop Biscuits p.13
     (use rice flour)
     w/ Strawberries

Day 1

Breakfast: Cooked Oatmeal Cereal p.3
w/ raisins
Banana

Lunch: Cream of Bean Soup p.70
Rye Crackers p.152
Grapes

Dinner: Stuffed Peppers p.62
Green Leafy Salad*
Cantaloupe

Day 3

Breakfast: Grape Nuts (Use Kamut flour) p.4
Blackberries

Lunch: Tuna Salad p.100
Crispy Potato Wedges p.86
Kamut Sourdough Bread p.26
w/Fig Butter p.145

Dinner: Chicken & Dumplings p.35
Tossed Salad p.100
Blueberry Pie p.138

Day 2

Breakfast: Whole Grain Pancakes p.6
Tangerine

Lunch: Kale Soup p.74
Spelt Thins p.153

Dinner: Steamed Asparagus p. 90
Tropical Turkey Salad p.97
Dinner Rolls p.27
Sour Cherry Pie p.138

Day 4

Breakfast :   Cracked Barley Cereal p.3
Raspberries

Lunch: Oven Fried Fish p.59
w/ Sourdough Rice Bread p.26
Grapefruit

Dinner: Cabbage Rice Casserole p.33
Green Leafy Salad*
Peach Pie p.139
w/ Coconut Pie Crust p.140

*Lettuce is one food that seldom causes reactions. You may be able to use lettuce every day.
We suggest you rotate between varieties of lettuce.

Day 1

Breakfast: Rye Bread, toasted p.27
Mango

Lunch: Bean Patties p.55
Green Leafy Salad*
Pumpkin Bars p.118

Dinner: Meat Pies p.38
Carrot Sticks
Oatmeal Cake p.111
Pears

Day 2

Breakfast: Cooked Kasha p.3
w/ Apple Juice
Apple

Lunch   Quick Drop Biscuits p.13
w/Turkey Gravy p.34
Sweet & Sour Broccoli-
Cauliflower Salad p.95
Rhubarb Crisp p.133

Dinner: Dorisa's Pigs in a Blanket p.80
Spinach Apple Salad p.99
Bran Muffins p.16
Apple Dessert p.127

Day 3

Breakfast: Blueberry Pancakes p.6

Lunch: Tuna Crunch Sandwich p.78
w/Kamut Bread p.27
Peas & Baby Potatoes p.89

Dinner: Stuffed Baked Potatoes p.88
Tossed Salad p.100
Frozen Blueberries

Day 4

Breakfast: Cooked Millet p.3
(Make extra for lunch)
Strawberries

Lunch: Fried Millet p.7
Green Leafy Salad*
Barley Cookies p.121

Dinner: Corn Bread p.19
w/ Ground Beef Gravy
using a *(day 4)* flour p.34
Berry Crisp p.129

*Lettuce is one food that seldom causes reactions. You may be able to use lettuce every day. We suggest you rotate between varieties of lettuce.

Breakfasts
and
Beverages

*Blueberry topping on pancakes is a most
delicious way to start the day!*

Hot Breakfast Cereals

Try cracking your own grains in the Vita-Mix (dry pitcher) or blender. You may need to vary cooking time with fineness of cracking process.

Bring liquid to a boil. If desired add a **pinch of salt** and $1/4$ **tsp. stevia**. Add grains, stirring until boiling and slightly thickened. Cover and simmer for the recommended time. Amaranth tends to clump to the bottom as it absorbs liquid. Stir it up several times during cooking time.

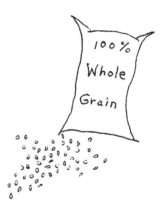

Tip: Various puffed grains are available at food co-ops, health food stores, and supermarkets for use as cold cereal for breakfast.

Grain - (1 cup)	Liquid	Cooking Time
Amaranth:	4 cups	45 min. to 1 hour
Barley, rolled:	2 cups	10 minutes
cracked:	$3^1/2$ cups	20 minutes
Buckwheat, Kasha:	$3^1/2$ cups	20 minutes
grits:	$3^1/2$ cups	20 minutes
Bulgur:	3 cups	30 minutes
Kamut, cracked:	$3^1/2$ cups	20 minutes
Millet:	3 cups	30 minutes
Oats, rolled, regular:	2 cups	15 minutes
steel cut:	3 cups	20 minutes
Quinoa:	3 cups	30 minutes
Cream of Rice:	3 cups	45 minutes
Spelt, rolled:	2 cups	15 minutes
cracked:	$3^1/2$ cups	20 minutes

Serve with <u>fruit</u>, <u>fruit juice</u>, <u>milk</u>, <u>nut milk,</u> or <u>rice milk</u>.

Tips for cracking your own grains using the dry pitcher of Vita-Mix: Use variable speed of 8.

Kamut:	approximately	30 seconds
Barley:	"	25 seconds
Rice:	"	20 seconds
Spelt:	"	10 seconds

Barley cereals are delicious with $1/4$ cup unsweetened coconut added at the end of cooking time.

GRANOLA
(day 1)
Combine:
2 cups rolled oats
$^{1}/_{2}$ cup oat bran

Mix:
$^{1}/_{4}$ cup grape juice
2 Tbsp. olive oil
$^{1}/_{2}$ tsp. stevia

Stir into rolled oats.
Bake at 325° F. for 45 minutes.
Stir every 15 minutes.
Add $^{1}/_{4}$ cup raisins.

Serves 4 - 6

Hint:
Who says pancakes have to have syrup on them? They are a delicious finger food without topping, if eaten warm, fresh off the griddle.

GRAPE NUTS
(day 2 or 1)
1 egg, optional or 1 Tbsp. water
3 cups spelt or oat flour
2 tsp. stevia
1 cup rolled spelt or oats
$^{1}/_{2}$ tsp. salt
2 tsp. soda
1 tsp. cream of tartar
2 cups apple or grape juice, or water
1 tsp. maple flavoring

Mix all ingredients.
Bake in 8 x 12" pan at 350° F. for 35 minutes.
Allow to cool.
Crumble and put on cookie sheets in thin layer, or put through a grape nut screen.
Stir occasionally and mash with fork during baking to make crumbs finer.
Bake crumbs in 250° F. oven until dry and crunchy.
Crack oven door open with spoon handle in top edge of oven door to allow steam to escape.
May be stored at room temperature up to 1 week.

BUCKWHEAT PANCAKES
(day 2)

In blender, process:
1¼ cups apple juice or water
3 Tbsp. olive oil
1 cup buckwheat flour
1 tsp. baking powder
½ tsp. salt
½ tsp. stevia

Whiz until just blended and pour onto hot greased griddle.
Turn pancakes once.   Yields 8 - 10 small pancakes

BUCKWHEAT MILLET PANCAKES

In blender, process:
2 Tbsp. olive oil
1 cup apple juice or water
¾ cup buckwheat flour
¼ cup millet flour
2 tsp. baking powder
½ tsp. stevia

Whiz until just blended. Pour onto hot greased griddle.
Turn pancakes once.
Delicious served with apple butter or blueberry topping.
                    Yields 8 - 10 small pancakes

RICE PANCAKES
(day 4)

In blender, process:
¼ cup olive oil
1½ cups fruit juice or water
2 tsp. baking powder
½ tsp. cream of tartar
½ tsp. salt
1 tsp. vanilla
1½ cups brown rice flour
½ tsp. stevia
1 tsp. guar gum

Scrape sides. Blend on medium speed until just combined.
Pour onto hot greased griddle. Turn once. Stir batter each time before pouring. Tastes best hot off the griddle.

Hint:
For quick pancakes in the morning: The night before combine all dry ingredients in a covered container. Measure liquids into blender. Next morning preheat griddle, blend ingredients to-gether, and you are eating in a jiffy.

OLD MILL OF
GUILFORD
WATER GROUND

BUCKWHEAT
FLOUR

5

BLUEBERRY PANCAKES
(day 3)

Blend in blender:
1 egg or $1/2$ tsp. guar gum + $1/2$ cup water
3 Tbsp. olive oil
1 tsp. vanilla

Add to blender:
$1\frac{1}{2}$ cups water	$1\frac{1}{2}$ cups kamut or spelt flour
2 tsp. baking powder	$1/2$ tsp. soda
$1/2$ tsp. cream of tartar	$1/2$ tsp. salt
1 tsp. stevia	

Blend on medium speed until just combined.
Stir in 1 cup blueberries.
Pour onto hot greased griddle, turning once.

Hint:
Olive oil works great to grease griddle for most pancakes. You may need to use butter with gluten free flour as it tends to stick more.

WHOLE GRAIN PANCAKES
(day 2)

$1/2$ cup olive oil	2 cups spelt or kamut flour
2 cups apple juice or water	1 Tbsp. baking powder
1 tsp. salt	$1/2$ tsp. stevia

In blender combine all ingredients until just mixed.
Pour onto hot greased griddle, turning once.

Makes 10 - 12 pancakes

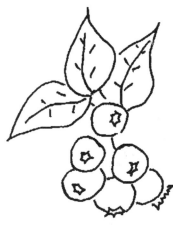

BLUEBERRY PANCAKE TOPPING

Heat until just beginning to boil:
3 cups blueberries
3 Tbsp. white grape juice concentrate or 3 Tbsp. water and 1 tsp. stev

Blend in blender until smooth.

Stir in:
1 cup blueberries

Serve warm.

FRIED MILLET

(day 4)
(REPLACES FRIED CORNMEAL MUSH)

Bring to a boil:
3 cups water
1/4 tsp. salt

Add:
1 cup millet

Bring to a boil and simmer 30 minutes, covered.
Stir well to rupture grains so they stick together.
Pour into greased bread pan.
Cool.
Slice 1/2" thick when ready to fry.

In heated skillet, put:
2 Tbsp. olive oil

Add millet slices.
Fry on both sides until crisp.
Serve plain or with apple butter.

Variation:

OVEN FRIED MILLET:

Put olive oil on both sides of millet slices, and place in cake pan.
Bake at 425° F. for 25 minutes.
Turn and bake 25 minutes longer or until crisp on the outside.

Hint: Don't know what to do with leftover cooked cereals? Try slicing and frying them for a delicious treat.

*Food
for Thought:*
*Don't wait for your
ship to come in.
Swim out to
meet it.*

7

CABBAGE-CARROT VITA DRINK

In Vita-Mix place:
2¹/₂ cups water
3 apples, chunked, stem and blossom end removed
3 - 4 cups cabbage, coarsely chopped
1 large carrot, chunked

Process on high until smooth.
Serve immediately.

Flax seed oil is an Omega 3 essential fatty acid and is believed to be very beneficial to our health. The Green Vita Drink is a delicious way to incorporate it into your diet.

GREEN VITA DRINK

If you have a Vita-Mix, try this for a delicious pick-me-up in the morning or all day.

3 cups grapes, seedless or seeded
1¹/₂ cups water
2 carrots, cut in 1 inch pieces
3 sweet apples, quartered, with stem and blossom end removed
1 banana
3 Tbsp. flax seed oil, optional
1 lemon, optional
1 orange, optional
2 - 3 large handfuls greens of your choice: lots of kale, romaine lettuce, spinach, and curly endive; small amounts of beet greens, dandelion, parsley, and celery

Put everything in Vita-Mix pitcher in order given, except greens.
Process on high.
Add greens through hole in lid while processing.
Best and most nutritious if served immediately, but will keep 2 - 3 days.

ALMOND MILK
(day 2)

Combine and soak overnight:
1 rounded cup whole, raw almonds
2 cups boiling apple juice or water

Next morning place nuts and liquid in blender.

Add:
2 cups water
$^{1}/_{8}$ tsp. salt
1 Tbsp. olive oil
$^{1}/_{2}$ tsp. vanilla, optional

Blend 2 - 3 minutes until smooth.
Strain through strainer or cheesecloth, squeezing or stirring liquid out
of pulp. Chill.   Makes about $^{3}/_{4}$ quart

Note: Pulp can be used in cake or bread.
It is delicious in oatmeal cake (page 111).

RICE MILK
(day 4)

Place in blender or Vita-Mix:
3 cups water
1 cup cooked rice
2 Tbsp. olive oil
$^{1}/_{2}$ tsp. liquid stevia
1 tsp. vanilla, optional
$^{1}/_{4}$ tsp. salt

Process until blended.
Strain through a fine strainer. (Use pulp in cakes or soups).

CAROB RICE MILK

To 1 cup rice milk, add:
$1^{1}/_{2}$ tsp. carob powder or to taste
$^{1}/_{4}$ tsp. stevia

SOY MILK

(day 1)

The simplest way is buying soy milk, but you can make your own.

Soak for 24 hours:
1 cup soybeans (less than one year old)
2$\frac{1}{2}$ cups water

Drain soybeans.
Rinse 1 time and add 2 cups water.
Bring to a boil and simmer, covered, for 1 hour.
Pour into blender.
Add 1$\frac{1}{2}$ cups water. Liquefy and strain through cheesecloth or strainer.
Add pinch of salt, $\frac{1}{2}$ tsp. vanilla, and 1 Tbsp. olive oil.

Yields about 1 quart

Note: For a thick creamy milk suitable for yogurt, blend in the Vita-Mix and use as is without straining.

Freezing mint tea:
In the summer, just before flower buds open, cut tea. Wash and allow water to evaporate. Pull leaves off stems and freeze in plastic bags or containers. Discard stems. We like this better than dried tea.

PERKED GARDEN TEA

For a quick refreshing break
In automatic coffee maker place:
10 cups cold water

Place in coffee filter:
1 cup frozen mint tea leaves (see side note), packed
1 tsp. stevia leaves

Perk as you would coffee.

ZUCCHINI MILK

(day 3)
Use in place of milk in cereal or pumpkin pie

In blender, process:
4 cups peeled zucchini chunks
$\frac{2}{3}$ cup water
$\frac{1}{4}$ tsp. stevia

Liquefy in blender.
Pour into saucepan and bring just to a boil.   Cool.
Refrigerate up to 4 days or freeze.

Breads

*Deborah works out her sourdough bread dough
to fit into the pans.*

QUICK DROP BISCUITS

(day 2 or 4)

2 cups spelt flour or 2$\frac{1}{2}$ cups rice flour
4 tsp. baking powder
1 tsp. cream of tartar
$\frac{1}{8}$ tsp. salt
3 Tbsp. olive oil
$\frac{7}{8}$ cup apple juice or water

Mix just until flour disappears.
Immediately drop by spoonfuls on cookie sheet.
Bake at 375° F. for 10 - 12 minutes.
Serve with gravy, fruit, apple butter, or jam.

Food for Thought: We take for granted the things that we should be thankful for.

SWEET POTATO BISCUITS

(day 2)

Beat together until well mixed:
1 cup cooked sweet potatoes, mashed
$\frac{1}{4}$ cup olive oil

Dissolve:
$\frac{1}{2}$ tsp. soda in $\frac{3}{4}$ cup water

Add to potato mixture.

Combine and add:
1$\frac{1}{2}$ cups spelt flour
1 Tbsp. baking powder
$\frac{1}{2}$ tsp. cream of tartar
1 tsp. salt
$\frac{1}{2}$ tsp. stevia, optional

Mix just until flour disappears.
Immediately drop by spoonfuls on cookie sheet.
Bake at 400° F. for about 15 minutes.
Serve plain or with strawberry jam.   Yields 12 biscuits

APPLE MUFFINS

1 banana, mashed
1/4 cup olive oil
1/2 cup apple juice or water
1/2 cup applesauce
1 3/4 cups spelt flour
1/4 cup oat or spelt bran

2 tsp. soda
1 tsp. cream of tartar
1/2 tsp. salt
3/4 tsp. cinnamon
1/4 tsp. nutmeg
1 cup chopped apples

Beat liquid ingredients together.
Add dry ingredients.
Mix until just moistened.
Fold apples in.
Fill greased muffin tins almost full.
Bake at 400° F. for 20 minutes.

BLACKBERRY MUFFINS
(day 4)

Mix together:
2 cups millet or rice flour
1/2 tsp. baking powder
1 tsp. soda
1/2 tsp. cream of tartar
1 1/2 tsp. cinnamon
2 tsp. stevia
1/2 tsp. salt
1 tsp. guar gum

Add:
3 Tbsp. olive oil
3/4 cup fruit juice or water

Mix just until combined.

Fold in:
2 cups fresh or thawed blackberries

Pour batter into greased muffin tin.

Bake at 400° F. for 20 - 25 minutes.

Yields 12 muffins

*Food
for Thought:*
*Patience is the
ability to idle
your motor when
you feel like
stripping your
gears.*

BLUEBERRY BANANA MUFFINS

2 ripe bananas, mashed
½ cup olive oil
1 cup water
1½ cups quinoa flour
½ cup tapioca starch
¼ tsp. stevia

1 Tbsp. baking soda
1 tsp. cream of tartar
½ tsp. salt
1 cup blueberries
1 cup walnuts, chopped

Place all ingredients except blueberries and walnuts in mixing bowl in order given.
Mix and fold in blueberries and walnuts.
Fill greased muffin tin almost full.
Bake at 400° F. for 12 - 15 minutes

Yields 12 muffins

*Food
for Thought:
If someone speaks
badly of you, live
so no one will
believe it.*

BLUEBERRY MUFFINS
(day 3)

Beat together:
1 cup fruit juice or water

2 Tbsp. olive oil

Add:
2 cups kamut or spelt flour
½ tsp. salt
1 tsp. cinnamon
2 tsp. stevia

2 tsp. baking soda
1 tsp. cream of tartar
¼ tsp. nutmeg, optional

Mix until just moistened.

Fold in:
1 cup blueberries

Fill greased muffin tin almost full.
Bake at 400° F. for 20 - 25 minutes. Remove from pan immediately.

Yields 12 muffins

BRAN MUFFINS

(day 2)

Combine in order given:
$^1/_2$ cup olive oil
1 Tbsp. molasses or 2 tsp. maple flavor
2 eggs or 1 tsp. guar gum
$1^1/_2$ cups spelt or oat bran
2 cups spelt flour
$1^1/_2$ tsp. stevia
$1^1/_2$ tsp. baking powder
$^1/_4$ tsp. cream of tartar
2 tsp. baking soda dissolved in $^1/_4$ cup boiling water
$1^1/_2$ cups apple juice or water
$^1/_2$ cup raisins, optional

Mix until just moistened. Fill greased muffin tin almost full.
Bake at 375° F for 25 minutes.   Yields 16 muffins

PECAN MUFFINS

(day 2)

Beat:
2 eggs or $^1/_4$ cup water + 1 tsp. guar gum
1 cup apple juice or water
$^1/_4$ cup olive oil
1 tsp. vanilla

Add:
2 cups spelt or kamut flour
1 Tbsp. baking powder   1 tsp. stevia
1 tsp. cinnamon $^1/_4$ tsp. salt

Mix until dry ingredients are just moistened. Fill muffin tin $^2/_3$ full.

CRUMB TOPPING:

Combine:
2 Tbsp. olive oil $^3/_4$ cup same kind of flour as above
1Tbsp. water   pinch salt
$^1/_2$ tsp. stevia $^1/_4$ cup pecans, chopped

Sprinkle over muffins and press crumbs slightly into batter.
Bake at 350° F. for 25 - 30 minutes.   Yields 18 muffins

PUMPKIN MUFFINS

In medium bowl, combine:

1 cup oat or kamut flour
³/₄ cup buckwheat flour
1¹/₂ tsp. baking powder
1 tsp. soda
¹/₂ tsp. cream of tartar

1 tsp. cinnamon
¹/₄ tsp. ginger
¹/₄ tsp. nutmeg
¹/₂ tsp. salt
1 tsp. guar gum

In another bowl, combine:

1 cup canned pumpkin
2 Tbsp. olive oil

1 cup apple juice or water

Add the pumpkin mixture to the flour mixture. Stir until just moistened.
Batter should be lumpy.
Spoon batter into greased muffin tin.
Bake at 400° F. for 20 - 25 minutes.
Cool in muffin tin for 5 minutes.
Serve warm.   Yields 12 muffins

SWEET POTATO MUFFINS

(day 2)
Delicious!

In mixer bowl, beat:

1 cup mashed sweet potatoes
1 cup apple juice or water
1 egg, beaten, or ¹/₂ tsp. guar gum + 2 Tbsp. water
¹/₄ cup olive oil

Add and mix:

2 cups spelt flour
2 tsp. baking powder
1 tsp. stevia
1 tsp. cinnamon
¹/₂ tsp. nutmeg
¹/₂ tsp. salt

Fold in:

¹/₄ cup walnuts, chopped

Fill greased muffin tin.
Bake at 375° F. for 30 - 35 minutes.   Yields 12 muffins

Food for Thought:
For every minute you are angry with someone, you lose 60 seconds of happiness you can never get back.

BAKED DONUTS
(day 2)

In mixing bowl, mix:
2 eggs or 1 tsp. guar gum + $^1/_2$ cup water
1 tsp. stevia
$^1/_4$ cup olive oil
1 cup apple juice or water

Add:
5 cups spelt flour
1 Tbsp. baking powder
1 tsp. soda
$^1/_2$ tsp. cream of tartar
$^1/_2$ tsp. salt
1 tsp. cinnamon

Mix until well mixed.
Roll out dough to about $^1/_2$" thick on lightly floured surface.
Cut donuts with donut cutter dipped in flour.
Place donuts and donut holes on cookie sheet.
Brush with olive oil and sprinkle with cinnamon.
Bake at 425° F. for 8 - 10 minutes.

Food for Thought:
Worry is like a rocking chair; it gives you something to do, but you never get anywhere.

BEAN CORN BREAD

Beat:
4 eggs or $^1/_4$ cup applesauce
$^1/_4$ cup olive oil
1 cup apple juice or water

Add:
$1^1/_2$ cups yellow cornmeal
1 cup well cooked mashed beans; pinto, kidney, or black
$^1/_8$ tsp. salt
4 tsp. baking powder

Mix only until well blended. Pour into greased 9 x 9" pan.
Bake at 400° F. for 40 - 45 minutes.

CORN BREAD
(day 4)

2 cups cornmeal
5 tsp. baking powder
1 tsp. cream of tartar
$^3/_4$ tsp. salt
1 tsp. guar gum
$^1/_2$ tsp. stevia
$^1/_4$ cup olive oil
1$^1/_4$ cups water

Combine all ingredients.
Pour into greased 8 x 12" pan.
Bake at 400° F. for 30 minutes.

DIANE'S CINNAMON SWIRL BREAD
(day 2)

Beat together:
$^1/_2$ cup olive oil
2 cups almond or rice milk
2 eggs or $^1/_2$ cup water + 1 tsp. guar gum

Add and mix:
4 cups spelt flour
2 tsp. soda
1 tsp. salt
2 tsp. stevia
$^1/_2$ cup chopped walnuts

Divide $^1/_2$ of the batter into 2 greased loaf pans.

Sprinkle over batter:
1 Tbsp. cinnamon

Top with the rest of the batter.
Swirl batter with a knife to make a pretty cinnamon swirl through bread.
Bake at 350° F. for 55 minutes. Remove from pan and cool.

MILLET RICE SHORTBREAD
(day 4)

4 cups millet flour
2 cups rice flour
2 Tbsp. baking powder
1/2 tsp. salt
1/4 tsp. stevia
2 tsp. guar gum, optional

1 cup olive oil
2 1/2 cups juice or water
2 tsp. vanilla

Mix dry and wet ingredients separately.
Combine wet and dry ingredients and stir until just combined.
Quickly pour into greased 8 x 12" pan prepared ahead of time, and put in preheated oven.
Bake at 350° F. for 45 - 50 minutes.
Serve with peaches, strawberries, juice, or rice milk.

PUMPKIN BREAD

Beat:
1/2 cup olive oil
2 eggs or 1/4 cup water + 1 tsp. guar gum
1 cup mashed pumpkin
1/3 cup water

Add and mix well:
1 1/2 cups spelt flour
2 tsp. baking powder
1/2 tsp. cream of tartar
1 tsp. soda
1 tsp. stevia
1 tsp. cinnamon
1/2 tsp. nutmeg
1/2 tsp. cloves
1/2 tsp. salt
1/2 cup chopped nuts, optional

Pour into a greased loaf pan.
Bake at 350° F. for 60 - 65 minutes. Remove from pan and cool.

Whenever possible buy your grains from a supplier that has a fast turnover and keeps them under refrigeration. After you buy your grains store them in the refrigerator or freezer to maintain freshness. You might try getting your grains from a local farmer for better prices. If you can get them soon after harvest and store them in a cool place, you will be assured of fresh quality.

GLUTEN FREE BREAD (YEAST FREE)

(day 4)

Dissolve:
1/2 tsp. baking soda in 1 cup hot apple juice or water

Set aside.

In mixer bowl, combine:
2 beaten eggs or 1 tsp. guar gum and 1/4 cup water
2 cups brown rice flour
2 tsp. baking powder
2 Tbsp. olive oil

Add soda liquid. Mix until just moistened. Pour into greased loaf pan.
Bake at 350° F. for 45 minutes.   Yields 1 loaf

ZUCCHINI BREAD

(day 3)

Mix well:
3 eggs or 3/4 cup water + 2 tsp. guar gum
1 cup olive oil
1 Tbsp. vanilla

Add and mix:
3 1/2 cups kamut or spelt flour
1 Tbsp. baking powder
2 tsp. soda
1 tsp. stevia
1 Tbsp. cinnamon
1/2 tsp. nutmeg

Stir in:
3 cups shredded, unpeeled zucchini
1 cup chopped peanuts
1 cup raisins, optional

Divide in 2 greased loaf pans.
Bake at 350° F. for 1 hour. Remove from pan and cool.

Note: Frozen shredded zucchini can be used. Discard about half of the juice from the zucchini.

APPLE PULL APART BREAD

(day 2)

Dissolve 10 minutes:

1 cup warm water
2 Tbsp. warm apple juice concentrate
1 Tbsp. yeast

Add:

2 Tbsp. olive oil
1 tsp. salt
$3^1/_2$ cups spelt flour

Cover and let rise in a warm place $1^1/_2$ - 2 hours.
Divide dough in half. Cut each half in 16 pieces.
On a floured surface, roll each piece into $2^1/_2$" circles.
Put 1 tsp. apple filling on center of each circle.
Pinch edges together and seal, forming a ball.
Dip in $1/_4$ cup olive oil.
Place all balls, seam side down, in a greased angel food cake pan.
Sprinkle remaining apple filling over top.
Cover and allow to rise in a warm place 1 - $1^1/_2$ hours.
Bake at 350° F. for 35 - 40 minutes.
Cool 10 - 15 minutes.
Remove and place on wire rack to cool.

APPLE FILLING:

1 large, sweet apple, peeled and shredded
$1/_2$ cup pecans, chopped
$1/_2$ tsp. cinnamon

Stir together.

POTATO CINNAMON ROLLS

In mixing bowl, combine:
$1/4$ cup white grape juice concentrate, warm
$3/4$ cup hot mashed potatoes
$1^1/4$ cups warm water
1 Tbsp. yeast

Allow to rest 5 minutes.

Add:
$1/2$ cup olive oil
2 eggs or $1/4$ cup water + $1/2$ tsp. guar gum
2 tsp. salt
$6^1/2$ - 7 cups spelt flour

Cover and allow to rise 1 hour.
Divide dough in half.
On a floured counter, roll out into two 12" squares.
Brush olive oil over dough.

Sprinkle with:
$1/2$ cup chopped walnuts
1 tsp. cinnamon

Roll up jelly roll style.
Cut each roll into 9 pieces.
Place in baking pan.
Cover and allow to rise in a warm place for 1 - $1^1/2$ hours.
Bake at 350° F. for 35 - 40 minutes.

Spiritual Nugget:
God's grace is immeasurable;
His mercy inexhaustible;
His peace inexpressible.

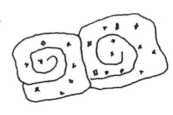

SOURDOUGH CINNAMON ROLLS

Use "Spelt Sourdough Bread" recipe and then follow directions for
"Potato Cinnamon Rolls", above.

SOURDOUGH STARTER

No commercial yeasts are used. As this mixture sits at room temperature it collects wild yeasts from the air.

Yeasts are simple one celled plants which float in the air most everywhere. When it bakes, the yeast plants are destroyed. If baked long enough, it should not smell yeasty.

Refrigeration preserves it. It needs to be brought to room temperature to reactivate the yeast.

Many people who cannot tolerate yeast breads can have sourdough breads.

Stir together using a plastic or wooden spoon in a <u>glass</u> bowl or container:
1/2 cup lukewarm water (95° - 105°)
1/2 cup spelt or other whole grain flour (room temperature)

Let set 10 - 15 minutes.

Stir in another:
1/2 cup lukewarm water (95° - 105°)
1/2 cup spelt or other whole grain flour (room temperature)

Cover loosely with plastic wrap.
Let set on counter 3 - 4 days. As it bubbles up, stir it back down with a <u>non-metal</u> spoon or spatula.
Any dark liquid that rises to the top should be stirred back in.
If at any time mold appears, remove it.
Discard starter if any pink color is detected.
Refrigerate starter at least 24 hours before using.

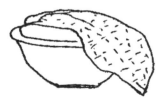

SPELT SOURDOUGH BREAD
(day 2)
Our Favorite!
Remove starter from refrigerator. Stir down dark liquid.

Measure out 1 cup of starter into <u>non-metal</u> bowl using a <u>non-metal</u> spoon (plastic or wooden).

[To remaining starter, add equal amounts of warm water and flour, 1/2 - 1 cup each, depending on how much you need to make adequate starter for the next time. Cover loosely and refrigerate. Do not use for 24 hours. <u>This is your starter for the next time you bake.</u> Use starter at least once a week. If you are unable to, freeze it in one cup portions or discard 1 cup and replenish starter with equal amounts of flour and water and refrigerate].

To make sponge, stir into starter with <u>non-metal</u> spoon or spatula:
1 1/2 cups warm water
3 1/2 cups spelt flour

Let set overnight, loosely covered - room temperature. Also allow flour to set out to come to room temperature.

Into sponge mixture, add:
4 Tbsp. white grape or apple juice concentrate, warm
1/3 cup olive oil
2 tsp. salt
1 cup flour

Beat just until mixed.

Add:
2 - 3 1/2 cups spelt flour

Quickly mix using dough hooks or bread kneader. (It may also be done by hand, but it tends to be sticky.)

Spelt bread should not be kneaded longer than necessary to knead flour in.

Cover and allow dough to rise 1 1/2 - 2 hours in a warm place.

Divide dough in half and shape into 2 loaves.

Place in greased loaf pans. Cover and allow to rise 1 - 1 1/2 hours in a warm place. Bake at 350° F. for 40 - 45 minutes.

Remove from pans. Cover with a towel. Do not slice until room temperature. Store in refrigerator or freezer.

Try making your own flour. Get your own flour mill or use the "dry" pitcher from your Vita-Mix blender. It will not be nearly as expensive, and the flour will be fresher if you make it as it is needed.

KAMUT SOURDOUGH BREAD
(day 3)

Follow "Spelt Sourdough Bread" recipe on preceding page, except substitute kamut flour for spelt, and use only 3 cups flour in sponge instead of 3¹/₂ cups.

DEREK'S SOURDOUGH RAISIN BREAD
Very Good!

Follow recipe for "Spelt Sourdough Bread" recipe on preceding page.

With the 1 cup of flour add:
> 1 tsp. stevia
> 1¹/₂ tsp. cinnamon

After all of the flour is worked in, work in 1¹/₂ cups raisins.

RICE SOURDOUGH BREAD
(This bread will be solid as there is not much gluten.)

Follow "Spelt Sourdough Bread" recipe on preceding page, using spelt flour for sponge. Next day, into sponge add 1 cup rice flour in place of spelt flour, and 3¹/₂ - 4¹/₂ cups rice flour in place of 2 - 3¹/₂ cups spelt flour.

SPROUTED GRAIN SOURDOUGH BREAD

Follow recipe for "Spelt Sourdough Bread" on preceding page, using flour for the sponge.
Next day, use 1 cup sprouted grain flour (page 28) in place of 1 cup spelt flour, and 1¹/₂ - 2 cups sprouted grain flour in place of 2 - 3¹/₂ cups spelt flour.

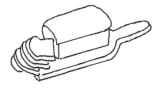

RYE BREAD
(Rye, a low gluten flour, will not rise like high gluten types.)
(day 1)

1¹/₂ cups warm water
3 Tbsp. warm white grape juice concentrate
1 Tbsp. yeast
2 tsp. salt
2 tsp. caraway seeds
¹/₄ cup olive oil
2 cups light rye flour
3 - 4 cups light rye flour (dark rye makes a heavy,
                                              strong tasting end product)

Dissolve yeast in warm water and juice for 10 minutes.
Add salt, caraway seeds, olive oil, and 2 cups flour.
Beat until smooth.
Slowly work in the rest of the flour.
Cover and allow to rise in a warm place for 2 hours.
Work into 2 loaves.
Place in greased loaf pans.
Allow to rise ¹/₂ - 1 hour.
Bake at 350° F. for 35 minutes.

Hint:
If the crust gets too hard when using glass pans to bake bread, lower the oven heat to 325° F.

Yields 2 loaves

DINNER ROLLS
(day 2)

In mixer bowl, mix and let set 5 minutes:
3 Tbsp. frozen apple juice concentrate in measuring cup, filling to
                        1 cup with hot water (mixture should be lukewarm)

1 Tbsp. yeast
¹/₂ tsp. salt

Add:
¹/₂ cup olive oil
1 Tbsp. vinegar
4 cups spelt flour

Mix and cover with plastic wrap. Refrigerate several hours or overnight.
Grease muffin tin and place 2 walnut sized balls of dough beside each other in each cup.
Let rise at room temperature for 3 - 4 hours.
Bake at 375° F. for 12 minutes.

Yields 10 rolls

For a delicious taste treat: Substitute 1 cup of flour with ¹/₂ cup of sprouted grain flour.

SPROUTED GRAIN BREAD

Divide evenly in 2 quart jars:
3 cups grain; wheat, spelt, or rye berries

Cover with lukewarm water and allow to soak overnight.
Next morning, drain water.
Put cheesecloth over opening with ring screwed on or use purchased sprouting jar covers.
Set upside down on the back of your sink with jars tilted a little to allow any water to drain off.
Rinse 3 - 4 times a day with room temperature water.

Two days later or when sprouts are $\frac{1}{8}$" long, they are ready to use.
Without rinsing again, spread grains out on large baking pans.
Dry in 250° F. oven until grains feel light and dry, stirring every hour.
Grind into flour.
(Refrigerate dried sprouted grain if you are not ready to use it.)

Mix together and allow to dissolve 5 minutes:
$1\frac{1}{2}$ cups warm water
$\frac{1}{4}$ cup warm white grape juice concentrate
2 Tbsp. yeast

Add and mix:
3 Tbsp. olive oil
1 tsp. salt
1 cup sprouted grain flour

Add:
2 - $2\frac{1}{2}$ cups sprouted grain flour

Knead until it leaves the sides of bowl. It will be sticky, but will absorb moisture while rising.
Cover and let rise 2 hours.
Work into 1 loaf. Place in greased pan.
Cover and allow to rise $1\frac{1}{2}$ hours.
Bake at 350° F. for 40 minutes.

Note: Any leftover sprouted grain flour can be used in place of any other flour. It will take less.

Sprouting grains for flour helps to release all the nutrients in the grain. It allows the proteins and carbohydrates to be used more efficiently by the body. Most grain allergy problems are caused by the gluten in the grain, and it is destroyed in the sprouting process.

Main Dishes

Diane presses the edges together on her "Meat Pies" to make a good seal.

BAKED BEANS

½ lb. ground beef
1 large onion, diced
6 cups cooked beans; kidney, pinto, turtle, etc.,drained and mixed
1 cup ketchup
½ cup water
1 Tbsp. vinegar
2 tsp. dry mustard
1 tsp. stevia
salt to taste

Brown meat. Add onion and continue cooking until onion is clear.
Stir in remaining ingredients. Pour into casserole. Cover.
Bake at 400° F. for 30 - 35 minutes or until bubbly.

Yields 10 - 12 servings

REFRIED BEANS

(day 3 or 1)
In large skillet, saute in ¼ cup olive oil:
1 medium leek or onion, chopped

Add:
4 cups drained, well cooked kidney or black beans
2 tsp. cumin
⅛ tsp. cayenne
salt and pepper to taste

Stir and mash beans with a fork or potato masher, leaving some
small chunks, until heated through.

BEAN BURRITOS

On warm tortilla, place any or all of the following:

refried beans, warm   minced onions
chopped lettuce or other greens   chopped tomatoes
salsa   shredded cheese or tofu

Roll up or place another tortilla on top and eat sandwich style.

Hint:
To avoid frustration have beans cooked ahead of time, because cooking time can be unpredictable. They can be frozen, stored refrigerated in their liquid for 3 - 5 days, or placed in jars boiling hot. Tighten lids securely. Make sure they seal. If they seal, they will keep at least 1 month in the refrigerator.

BEAN DIP

(day 1)

3 cups well cooked black turtle beans or kidney beans
$1/4$ cup liquid from cooking beans
2 cups stewed tomatoes, drained, optional
1 small onion, chopped

$1/4$ cup lemon juice
2 tsp. cumin
1 - 2 tsp. cayenne

2 tsp. chili powder
1 tsp. garlic powder
$1/4$ tsp. salt

Blend all ingredients, reserving one cup of beans.
Lightly mash the one cup beans.
Add:
$1/4$ cup red bell pepper, chopped

Add the one cup beans and red bell pepper to the blended beans.
Serve with tortilla chips.

Note: 1 - $1^1/_2$ cups tomato juice can be used in place of stewed tomatoes. Add more if too thick.

Tip: Hungry for bean dip, but allergic to corn? Try spreading it on rice cakes.

BROCCOLI RICE CASSEROLE

Bring to a boil and simmer 45 minutes:
4 cups chicken broth
4 cups water
2 cups cooked chicken, chopped
2 cups brown rice
1 tsp. salt

Add:
1 large bunch broccoli, chopped
$1/2$ tsp. nutmeg

Continue simmering 15 minutes or more.
Serve.

Want to cook your own beans because of the chemicals in the bought ones? Put dry beans in a large kettle and cover with water. Soak 6 hours or overnight. Drain. Cover with fresh water. Cover and bring to a boil. Simmer until tender, approximately 1 hour. Add more water if needed. Salt to taste. Drain and use in recipes, refrigerate, or freeze for later use.

CABBAGE BARLEY CASSEROLE

Bring to a boil and simmer, covered, for $1/2$ hour:
2 cups chicken or vegetable broth (page 147)
2 cups water
1 cup hulled barley
1 tsp. salt

Top with:
6 cups cabbage, chopped

Do not stir.
Cover and simmer $1/2$ hour longer.

Note: For (day 4) CABBAGE RICE CASSEROLE
Add $1/2$ lb. ground beef, browned, or $1/2$ lb. chunk beef.
Substitute beef broth or water for the chicken broth
and rice for barley.

Tip:
Not only is barley fairly high in protein, but it is also high in lysine, which makes it a more complete (usable) protein on its own.

CHICKEN SPAGHETTI

2 cups cooked chicken, chopped
2 cups celery, chopped
1 medium onion, chopped
$1/4$ cup green pepper, diced
1 Tbsp. hot pepper, diced
salt and pepper to taste
1 garlic clove, minced, or 1 tsp. garlic powder
16 oz. package whole grain spaghetti
2 cups cream soup (page 70)
8 oz. "Dairy Free Cheese", grated (page 146)

Cook spaghetti.
Mix all ingredients together. Sprinkle more cheese over top.
Bake in casserole at 350° F. for 1 hour.

Serves 8

EASY CHICKEN CASSEROLE
(day 3)

2 cups chicken broth
2 cups cooked chicken, chopped
4 cups cooked kidney or pinto beans
4 medium cooked potatoes, diced
3/4 tsp. salt

Combine in casserole. Cover.
Bake at 350° F. for 1 hour.

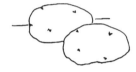

CHICKEN POTATO CASSEROLE
(day 3)

1 cup cooked chicken, chopped
5 medium, unpeeled potatoes, diced
2 cups chicken gravy

1 leek, chopped
1 stalk celery, chopped
1/2 tsp. salt

Stir all ingredients together.
Bake in covered casserole at 350° F. for 1 hour.

CHICKEN OR TURKEY GRAVY
(day 2 or 3)   (For day 3 use potato starch in place of clear jel.
Process in blender after boiling to eliminate lumps.)

(For over mashed potatoes, hash browns, rice, sweet potatoes, or bread)

2 cups chicken or turkey broth
1/4 cup cooked chicken or turkey, chopped
salt and pepper to taste

3 Tbsp. clear jel
1/2 cup water
1/2 tsp. sage

Bring broth and meat to a boil. Dissolve clear jel in water and stir into broth. Boil 1 minute, stirring constantly. Add seasonings.

Tip:
Potato starch can be stirred into browned hamburger. Then pour broth or tomato juice in and bring to a boil. Stir 1 - 2 minutes for gravy.

SALMON GRAVY

3 Tbsp. olive oil
1/2 cup rice flour
2 1/2 cups water

3/4 tsp. salt
dash pepper
1 - 15 oz. can salmon, drained

Heat oil. Add flour and stir until brown. Slowly add water and cook until thickened. Add remaining ingredients.

CHICKEN AND DUMPLINGS

(day 3)

In a large skillet, bring to a boil:
2 cups cooked chicken, chopped
3 cups broth or water
2 Tbsp. chives, chopped
2 stalks celery, chopped
1 tsp. salt
$1/8$ tsp pepper, optional

Meanwhile, mix:
2 cups kamut or spelt flour
4 tsp. baking powder
$1/2$ tsp. salt
$3/4$ cup water

Quickly drop dough by small spoonfuls over chicken.
Cover.
Simmer for 15 - 20 minutes.
Don't lift lid while cooking.
Serve immediately.

*Food
for Thought:
If you fill your heart
with regrets of yester-
day and the worries of
tomorrow, you
have no "today" to
be thank-
ful for.*

Serves 8

CHICKENY GARDEN CASSEROLE

In large casserole, combine:
3 cups potatoes, unpeeled, cubed
2 cups parsnips, cubed
2 cups carrots, cubed
$1^1/2$ cups cooked chicken, diced
1 cup broth or water
1 tsp. salt

Bake covered at 350° F. for 1 hour and 15 minutes.

When done add:
$1/2$ cup chives, cut fine
2 cups greens, chopped

Optional:
Use 2 cups broth in place of one cup broth, and add $1/3$ cup rice,
barley, or millet. Put the grain in the bottom of casserole before adding the other ingredients. Delicious!

CHICKEN POT PIE

(day 3)

4 cups potatoes, diced
1 stalk celery, chopped
1 small leek, thinly sliced
$1/2$ cup peas
$1/4$ cup water

Bring to a boil and simmer 15 - 20 minutes or until vegetables are tender.

Add:
1 cup cooked chicken, chopped
2 cups chicken gravy
1 tsp. salt

CRUST:

$1/4$ cup olive oil
$3^1/4$ cups kamut flour
$1^1/2$ tsp. soda
$1/2$ tsp. cream of tartar
$1/4$ tsp. salt
1 cup water

Combine oil and dry ingredients.
Slowly add water while stirring.
Makes enough for top and bottom crust.
Roll out bottom crust and place in 8 x $1^1/2$" round pan.
Pour in vegetables.
Top with top crust.
Trim, pressing both crusts together, and flute.
Make slits in top crust for steam to escape.
Bake at 375° F. for 40 minutes.

ITALIAN MACARONI

Cook according to package directions:
1/2 lb. spelt macaroni

Meanwhile brown:
1/2 lb. ground turkey

Add and cook until clear:
1 onion, diced
1 clove garlic, minced fine

Add:
1 stalk celery, chopped
1 quart canned tomato chunks
1 tsp. salt
1 tsp. oregano
1/8 tsp. pepper, optional

Simmer 5 minutes.
Stir into cooked macaroni. Pour into casserole.
Bake at 350° F. for 35 minutes, or 1 hour if refrigerated. Serves 10 - 12

ITALIAN MEAT SAUCE

Saute in 1/4 cup olive oil:
1 clove garlic, minced
1 small onion, diced

Add:
1 lb. ground beef or venison, browned
1 quart canned tomato chunks
1 tsp. salt
1 tsp. oregano
1/2 tsp. basil
1/8 tsp. pepper

Simmer uncovered for 45 minutes.

Add:
1/2 cup sliced mushrooms

Simmer 15 minutes longer.
Serve over spaghetti or noodles (10 oz. before cooked).

Serves 6

Food for Thought: The only people we should try to get even with are those who have helped us.

LENTILS

(day 3)

4 cups chicken broth
2 cups lentils
$^3/_4$ tsp. salt
5 "Sheltons" chicken or turkey franks, sliced

Simmer broth, lentils, and salt, covered, for $^1/_2$ hour.
Add franks and continue simmering 10 - 20 minutes.

Hint "Sheltons Franks" do not contain sugar, nitrates, or preservatives. They are available in health food stores or food co-ops.

MEAT PIES

(day 1 use oat flour)

FILLING:

1 lb. venison or ground beef, browned
1 cup cooked black turtle beans, mashed
$^2/_3$ cup pizza sauce or water
$^1/_2$ tsp. salt
$^1/_8$ tsp. pepper

1 medium onion, chopped
1 clove garlic, minced
2 Tbsp. parsley
$^1/_2$ tsp. ginger

Combine all ingredients.

BISCUITS:

2 Tbsp. olive oil
2 tsp. baking powder
$^1/_4$ tsp. salt

$2^2/_3$ cups spelt or oat flour
$^1/_4$ tsp. cream of tartar
$^3/_4$ cup + 2 Tbsp. water
($^2/_3$ cup water for oat flour)

Hint:
When making meat pies make a double batch of filling. Leftover filling is delicious on rice tortillas.

Mix all ingredients together.
Roll out $^1/_8$" thick.
Cut into 3 - 4" circles.
Place $^1/_2$ of circles on cookie sheet.
Squeeze meat mixture into a ball about $^1/_2$" smaller than circle.
Place ball in the center.
Pat top circles into slightly larger circles.
Place over filling.
Seal edges with water and pinch edges together.
Prick top of pies with a fork.
Bake at 375° F. for 15 minutes.

Serves 6 - 8

NOODLES

BARLEY:
(day 4)
1³⁄₄ - 2 cups barley flour
¹⁄₄ tsp. salt, optional
³⁄₄ cup water

OAT:
(day 1)
1³⁄₄ - 2 cups oat flour
¹⁄₄ tsp. salt, optional
¹⁄₂ cup water

RICE:
(day 4)
2 cups rice flour
¹⁄₄ tsp. salt, optional
²⁄₃ cup water
1 tsp. guar gum

KAMUT:
(day 3)
2 cups kamut flour
¹⁄₄ tsp. salt, optional
³⁄₄ cup water

RYE:
(day 1)
2 cups light rye flour
¹⁄₄ tsp. salt, optional
²⁄₃ cup water

SPELT:
(day 2)
2-2¹⁄₄ cups spelt flour
¹⁄₄ tsp. salt, optional
³⁄₄ cup water

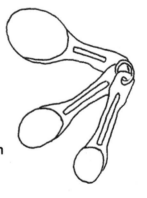

Measure flour and salt into bowl.

Slowly pour water in while stirring with a fork.

When it is too thick to stir, knead with hands. Dough should be stiff.

Cover dough and allow to set ¹⁄₂ hour.

Put through pasta maker, or divide dough in 4 parts.

On floured surface, roll each part out as thin as possible.

(Oat, rice, and barley are difficult to roll. You may want to cut them in strips without hanging to dry or rolling up like jelly roll.)

Hang over drying rack and allow to dry ¹⁄₂ - 1 hour.

Flour each side if sticky.

Roll up like jelly roll, and cut noodles desired width.

Spread out to finish drying on counter.

Refrigerate and use within 4 days, or freeze.

Note: For large batches of noodles, use a dough hook or Bosch to combine ingredients.

Cooking takes about 5 - 10 minutes, depending on width of noodles and flour used.

Or bring water to a boil. Add noodles. Return to boiling, cover, and remove from heat. Let set 20 - 25 minutes.

DRESSING-NOODLE CASSEROLE
(day 2)
Delicious!

NOODLES:

1 cup cooked turkey, chopped
4 cups turkey broth
1 lb. spelt noodles

2$\frac{1}{2}$ cups water
1 tsp. salt

Bring turkey, broth, water, and salt to a boil.
Add noodles and bring to a boil again.
Turn heat off. Cover and let set 25 minutes.
Meanwhile make dressing.
After noodles are done, drain extra broth off into dressing.
Spread noodles in bottom of casserole.

DRESSING:

4 cups spelt bread crumbs
1 stalk celery, chopped
1 Tbsp. olive oil
1 tsp. sage

$\frac{1}{4}$ cup sliced mushrooms
1 small onion, chopped,
　optional
$\frac{1}{2}$ tsp. salt

Stir together with broth drained from noodles.
Spread dressing on top of noodles.
Bake, covered, at 350° F. for 1 hour.
Uncover and bake 10 minutes longer.

Hint: Dressing may be spread over mashed potatoes in place of noodles. Add turkey broth to dressing until bread crumbs are well soaked.

MILLET STEW

4$\frac{1}{2}$ cups broth or water
1 cup millet
1 onion, chopped
3 medium potatoes, diced
1 large carrot, diced

$\frac{1}{2}$ cup celery, chopped
$\frac{1}{2}$ tsp. thyme
1 tsp. salt
pepper to taste

Mix all **ingredients** in 2$\frac{1}{2}$ quart casserole.
Bake **at** 350° F. for 1$\frac{1}{4}$ - 1$\frac{1}{2}$ hours.

OAT FLOUR PIZZA CRUST
(day 1)

Combine:
3¹/₂ cups oat flour
2 Tbsp. baking powder
1¹/₂ tsp. cream of tartar
¹/₄ tsp. salt
5 Tbsp. olive oil

Add:
1¹/₃ cups water

Spread onto greased 14" pizza pan.
Bake at 375° F. for 10 minutes.

Top with pizza sauce (page 165), browned ground venison, chopped onion, chopped peppers, and *(day 1)* shredded "Dairy Free Cheese".
(page 146)

Bake at 350° F. for 20 minutes.

SOURDOUGH PIZZA CRUST
Our favorite!

Combine in bowl:
¹/₂ cup starter (page 24)
¹/₂ cup warm water
1 cup spelt flour

Cover and allow to rest 8 - 10 hours or overnight.

Add and mix:
¹/₄ cup olive oil
1¹/₂ tsp. salt

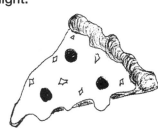

Gradually add:
1³/₄ cups spelt flour

Press into pizza pan.
Let rise 1 hour.
Prebake at 375° F. for 10 minutes.
Add toppings.
Return to oven and bake 20 minutes longer.

QUINOA DRESSING

(day 3)

3 cups chicken broth or water
1½ cups quinoa
1 Tbsp. olive oil
1 medium onion, chopped

1 stalk celery, chopped
2 tsp. sage
½ tsp. salt
dash pepper

In saucepan, bring chicken broth to a boil. Add quinoa and simmer, covered, 20 - 25 minutes.
Meanwhile saute onion and celery in oil for 10 minutes.
Add spices and mix into quinoa.
Serve.

Stuffing for poultry: Stuff poultry with dressing and roast as usual.

Serves 4 - 6

Why cook your own beans? Bought canned beans may contain sugar, corn syrup, and various chemicals such as calcium chloride and disodium EDTA.

FRIED RICE AND BEANS

Frying the rice gives this dish a delicious flavor!

2 Tbsp. olive oil
1 onion, chopped
1 garlic clove, minced
⅔ cup brown rice, uncooked
2 cups chicken broth
1 tsp. salt
1 tsp. cumin
1 tsp. oregano
3 cups cooked black beans

In a large skillet, saute onions and garlic in hot oil for 3 - 4 minutes.
Add rice and saute 3 - 4 minutes.
Add chicken broth and salt.
Bring to a boil and simmer, covered, for 30 minutes.
Add beans and spices.
Simmer 10 more minutes.

Serves 6 - 8

RICE FISH CASSEROLE

1 lb. fish, cut in 1" cubes
5 cups brown rice, cooked
1 cup peas, thawed
2 Tbsp. green pepper, chopped
1 Tbsp. dried parsley
$1/2$ tsp. salt
pepper to taste
$1/2$ cup water

Mix all ingredients together.
Bake in covered casserole at 350° F. for 1 hour.

Serves 6 - 8

Food for Thought:
Gossip is like feathers in the wind – irretrievable.

SPAGHETTI

1 lb. ground venison
1 large onion, diced
1 clove garlic, minced
10 oz. spelt spaghetti
1 cup cooked, diced carrots
1 quart spaghetti or pizza sauce
salt to taste
$1/2$ tsp. basil

Cook spaghetti according to package directions.
Brown meat.
Add onion and garlic and cook until clear.
Combine all ingredients.
Spaghetti and sauce should be fairly thin, as spaghetti will absorb more moisture while baking.
Bake, covered, at 350° F. for 1 hour.

RICE TORTILLAS

Blend together in blender:

1½ cups cold water
1¾ cups brown rice flour
½ tsp. salt

2 Tbsp. olive oil
1 egg, optional

Pour onto hot greased skillet. Stir each time you pour a new batch.

Makes 12 tortillas

Note: For corn tortillas, omit rice flour and add 1 cup spelt or kamut flour and ½ cup cornmeal.

Choose your own toppings:
Browned ground beef with pizza sauce or tomato paste
Chicken or turkey with a starch thickener and water
Mashed beans or refried beans
Salsa
Chopped tomatoes
Chopped lettuce
Minced onions
Shredded cheese

Also delicious with "Meat Pies" filling (page 38).

For moist, "just right" rice: In a 2½ qt. casserole, put 6 cups water, 2 cups brown rice, and 1 tsp. salt. Bake covered at 350° F. for 1½ hours.

SKILLET TUNA POTATO CASSEROLE
(day 3)

4 Tbsp. olive oil
4 medium potatoes, sliced
1 - 6 oz. can tuna, drained
½ cup water
1 - 4 oz. can mushrooms, undrained, optional

In skillet, cook potatoes in olive oil until just soft.
Add rest of ingredients and heat through.
Add salt and pepper to taste.

TURKEY BARLEY STEW

In skillet, saute in 2 Tbsp. olive oil:
2 cups cooked turkey, chopped
1 onion, chopped

Transfer to crock pot and add:
1 qt. water	2 cups tomato juice
1 large carrot, diced	1 stalk celery, thinly sliced
2 tsp. salt	1/2 tsp. oregano
1/2 tsp. paprika	1/4 tsp. pepper

Cover and cook on low for 4 - 5 hours.

Add:
2 cups green beans
1/4 cup hulled barley
2 cups corn, optional

Cover and cook 2 hours longer or until barley and vegetables are done.

Tip: When buying turkey, be sure it is not basted. Local farmers are a good source. Buy several at Thanksgiving. Roast, pick meat off bones, and freeze for tasty dishes throughout the year. It may also be cooked, picked off bones, and frozen.

RICE STIR FRY

1/4 cup olive oil	salt and pepper to taste
1 clove garlic, minced	1 Tbsp. soy sauce
1 small onion, minced	1 cup cooked chicken, diced
1/4 tsp. ginger	5 cups cooked rice, cooled
1/8 tsp. cayenne pepper	3 cups dandelion, finely chopped

Place oil in wok or large heavy skillet.   When oil is hot add garlic, onion, spices, and chicken.
Stir constantly on high heat for 1 minute. Turn heat to medium. Add rice.
Crumble to eliminate lumps.   Stir for 2 minutes.
Add greens. Stir for about 3 minutes or until greens are tender-crisp.
Serve immediately.

Dandelion may be substituted with kale, mustard greens, or turnip greens.
Remove stems.   Serves 6 - 8

FISH STIR FRY

Mix and set aside:
Sauce:
¹/₂ cup water
2 Tbsp. soy sauce
2 Tbsp. lemon juice
1 Tbsp. cornstarch
¹/₂ tsp. dry mustard
dash pepper
1 tsp. ginger

Preheat in skillet on medium heat:
1 Tbsp. olive oil

Add and stir fry 4 minutes:
1 lb. fresh asparagus, cut in ³/₄" pieces
1 clove garlic, minced
1 large sweet red pepper, cut in ¹/₂" pieces

Remove vegetables.

1 Tbsp. olive oil
1 lb. fish, cut in 1" cubes

Stir fry fish in oil in heavy skillet for 6 minutes, turning every 2 minutes. Stir fry only half of the fish at a time. Remove.
Put vegetables back in skillet and stir in sauce.
Heat until bubbly.
Add fish and serve immediately over a bed of rice.

Allergic to soy?
Omit soy sauce and replace water with meat broth and 1 tsp. salt.

Note: Asparagus can be replaced with cauliflower, carrots, onions, celery, and snow peas.

Hint:
For variety, add sliced water chestnuts to any stir fry. Add with the vegetables.

46

SPRING STIR FRY

(Pictured on front cover.)
Sauce:
2 Tbsp. cornstarch or arrowroot flour, dissolved in $\frac{1}{4}$ cup water
1 cup broth
2 Tbsp. soy sauce or 1 tsp. salt
1 Tbsp. lemon juice

In medium saucepan bring the broth to a boil.
Stir the rest of the ingredients in.
For cornstarch boil 1 - 2 minutes stirring constantly.   Set aside.
Turn burner off for arrowroot.

Hint:
When picking fresh dandelion, pick as early in the spring as possible for a milder green. Also: Try adding some to salads.

4 - 5 Tbsp. olive oil
$\frac{1}{2}$ to 1 cup cooked chicken - bite size
4 cups fresh vegetables of your choice, sliced in bite size pieces:
      carrots
      onions
      cauliflower
      celery
      broccoli
1 - 2 cups dandelion greens, chopped, or spinach

Saute chicken pieces in 2 Tbsp. of the oil.
Remove and add remaining oil and desired vegetables to pan in order of cooking time needed; carrots, onions, and cauliflower first. Toss a few minutes and add the rest.
Vegetables should be bright in color and tender-crisp. Do not overcook.
Add chicken and stir in sauce.
Add dandelion and heat until just bubbly.
Salt to taste.
Serve immediately over a bed of rice.

Note: In the summer omit dandelion greens and add peppers, zucchini, or snow peas before adding the chicken.

SPANISH RICE

$^1/_2$ lb. ground beef or venison, browned
1 cup uncooked brown rice
2 Tbsp. olive oil
1 small onion, chopped
1 clove garlic, minced
$^3/_4$ tsp. salt
2 large, peeled tomatoes, chopped
1 cup water
1 cup chicken broth
$^1/_3$ cup frozen peas
$^1/_3$ cup diced, cooked carrots

In a large skillet, saute rice in oil 4 - 5 minutes until lightly brown.
Add onion, garlic, and salt.
Cook on low heat until onion is clear.
Add meat, tomatoes and water.
Simmer, covered, until water is absorbed, about $^1/_2$ hour.
Stir in broth, peas, and carrots.
Cover and simmer until liquid is absorbed and rice is tender, about
15 minutes.   Yields 6 - 8 servings

Do not stir grains while cooking. It will rupture the cells and produce a starchy, sticky dish. One exception is amaranth, which needs stirring because it tends to clump to the bottom as it absorbs liquid.

BEAN & RICE STUFFED ZUCCHINI

Cut in half lengthwise and scoop out pulp:
1 large zucchini or 5 baby zucchinis

Combine:
1$^1/_2$ cups cooked pinto, black beans, or kidney beans
1 cup cooked rice $^1/_2$ cup carrots, finely diced
$^1/_4$ cup minced onion   1 medium tomato, chopped
$^1/_8$ tsp. garlic powder   1 tsp. salt
dash pepper $^1/_2$ tsp. basil
$^1/_2$ tsp. chili powder

Mix together and pile into zucchini. Bake covered, large zucchini at
375°F. for 1$^1/_2$ hours and baby zucchinis for 45 minutes to 1 hour.
Grate "Dairy Free Cheese" (page 146) over top and continue baking,
uncovered, until cheese is melted.

CHICKEN STUFFED ZUCCHINI

(day 3)

1 large zucchini
1 cup broth
2 cups cooked chicken, chopped
1 stalk celery, chopped
3 cups whole grain bread crumbs
$1/2$ tsp. ginger
$1/2$ tsp. sage
1 tsp. salt

Cut zucchini in half lengthwise.
Scoop out seeds and pulp and discard.
Mix all ingredients together and fill zucchini.
Bake covered at 375° F. for $1^1/2$ hours.

*Food
for Thought:
The choices we make
today will
usually affect
tomorrow.*

STUFFED ZUCCHINI

1 large zucchini
$1/2$ lb. ground venison or ground beef, browned
1 small onion, chopped
2 cups peeled tomatoes, chopped
1 cup whole grain bread crumbs
$1/2$ tsp. salt
$1/2$ tsp. sage
pepper to taste

Cut zucchini in half lengthwise and scoop out the pulp.
Mix the remaining ingredients and stuff zucchini.
Bake covered at 375° F. for $1^1/2$ - 2 hours, depending on size.
Slice crosswise in 2" pieces to serve.

POTATO-CARROT-PARSNIP SKILLET

Heat in skillet:
1 Tbsp. olive oil

Add:

2 cups carrots, 1" cubes	3 cups parsnips, 1" cubes
4 cups potatoes, 1" cubes	salt and pepper to taste

Cover and saute until tender-crisp, approximately 20 minutes.
Turn off heat.

Add:
1/2 cup parsley flakes

 Stir and let set covered 5 minutes before serving.

Note:
If you have leftovers, try adding them to cooked lentils.

Food for Thought:
Anger is a condition in which the tongue works faster than the brain.

UGALI

(The national dish of Kenya)

They cook it to a very thick consistency, then pour it out onto a plate for everyone to eat from.

You take a piece, roll it into a ball, punch a hole in, and scoop up Sakuma and eat "spoon" and all.

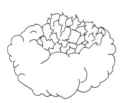

3 cups boiling water	1/2 tsp. salt
1 cup cold water	1/8 tsp. pepper
2 cups cornmeal	

Stir the cornmeal, salt, and pepper into the cold water.
Slowly pour the mixture into the boiling water, stirring constantly.
Continue stirring for 20 minutes until <u>very</u> thick and smooth.
Cover and leave on very low heat for 10 - 15 minutes to finish cooking.
Serve immediately while hot.

(continued on next page)

UGALI (continued from last page)

They may also be formed ahead of time.
Reduce cornmeal by $1/2$ cup. Allow ugali to cool a little. Make "spoons" as previously mentioned and place on baking pan.

Fill with **"SAKUMA"** and heat in 350° F. oven for 10 - 20 minutes.

Food for Thought:
To get out of a difficulty, one must usually go through it.

SAKUMA

3 Tbsp. oil
$2/3$ cup peeled tomatoes, chopped
salt and pepper to taste

1 onion, chopped
6 cups kale, finely chopped

Heat oil in large frying pan. Add onions and tomatoes. Saute about 3 minutes or until onions are clear. Reduce heat to low and add kale, salt, and pepper.
Cover and cook together 10 minutes if fixing ahead of time and reheating. Cook 20 - 25 minutes if serving immediately.

They also like ugali served with chicken:

6 Tbsp. olive oil
1 large tomato, diced
1 onion, chopped
1 frying chicken, cut up

Heat 3 Tbsp. oil in a large frying pan.
Fry chicken, single layer, until browned.
Place all of chicken in a kettle.

Heat 3 Tbsp. oil in skillet.
Add tomatoes and onions and saute for 2 - 3 minutes.
Pour over chicken and cover chicken with water.
Cook $3/4$ - 1 hour or until tender.
Remove chicken and place on platter to serve.
Broth is served in your bowl to dip ugali in.

RICE STUFFED ZUCCHINI

1 large zucchini for stuffing   1/2 lb. ground beef, browned
1/2 tsp. salt   1 Tbsp. onion
1/4 tsp. thyme   2 Tbsp. parsley, chopped, optional
2 cups cooked brown rice, cold

Cut large zucchini in half lengthwise and scoop out the pulp.
Mix the rest of the ingredients.
Stuff zucchini and bake covered at 375° F. for 1 1/2 hours.
Slice crosswise in 2" pieces to serve.

SPAGHETTI SQUASH CASSEROLE

(day 1)

1 spaghetti squash
1/2 lb. ground venison or beef
1 Tbsp. olive oil
1 medium onion, chopped
1 clove garlic, minced
2 large, peeled tomatoes, chopped
1 tsp. salt
pepper to taste
1 tsp. basil
1 tsp. oregano
1 cup whole grain bread crumbs

Cut spaghetti squash in half lengthwise.
Scoop out seeds.
Place halves cut side down in baking pan, adding 1 Tbsp. water to pan.
Cover with foil and bake at 350° F. for 1 1/2 hours or until soft.
Brown meat.
Add oil, onion, and garlic. Cook until clear.
Add tomatoes and simmer uncovered until most of liquid is gone.
Add seasonings.
Using fork, scoop out spaghetti strands and add to meat.
Add bread crumbs.
Pour into casserole.
Bake covered at 375° F. for 30 - 40 minutes.

Food for Thought:
Everyone needs to be loved, especially when they don't deserve it.

Meats

Fish and poultry, being a complete protein, are a good supplement to the diet, supplying B-vitamins, amino acids, and phosphorus.

BEAN PATTIES

(day 1)
Combine in blender:

2 cups well cooked or canned northern, navy, or pinto beans
1/4 cup water
1/2 cup onion, minced
3 Tbsp. olive oil

1/2 tsp. salt
1/4 cup fresh parsley leaves, minced
1/3 cup rolled oats

Blend. Add a little more water if too thick to blend.
Form into patties.
Heat an additional 2 Tbsp. olive oil in heavy skillet.
Add patties, cover, and cook until browned on both sides.

Serve with ketchup, salsa, or tomato and lettuce.

Serves 4

Beans, split peas, and lentils are high in fiber and protein, and can easily be used without meat in preparing a meal.

BAKED CHICKEN

(day 3)
4 leg quarters
1/4 cup olive oil
3/4 cup quinoa or rice flour
1 1/2 tsp. Italian seasoning
salt and pepper to taste

Combine flour and seasonings. Dip chicken in oil, then roll in flour
and seasonings. Place single layer on greased baking pan.
Bake uncovered at 350° F. for 1 1/4 - 1 1/2 hours.

CHICKEN BREASTS

2 boneless, skinless chicken breasts, rinsed and patted dry
1 Tbsp. olive oil
1 Tbsp. parsley
1 tsp. celery seed

1 Tbsp. lemon juice
1 tsp. Italian seasoning

Slice the chicken breasts in half so they are thinner.
Combine rest of ingredients.
Marinate chicken in mixture at least 1 hour or overnight.
Coat with quinoa flour, cornmeal, or rice flour.
Salt and pepper to taste.
Bake uncovered at 375° F. for 25 - 30 minutes.

CHICKEN HERB MARINADE

4 chicken breasts

Mix together:

4 Tbsp. olive oil

1 garlic clove, minced

1½ tsp. ground sage

¼ cup lemon juice

1½ tsp. rosemary

¼ tsp. pepper

Marinate chicken in mixture 4 - 8 hours.
Grill or roll in flour or crushed corn flakes, and bake uncovered at 350° F
for 1 hour.

LEMON MARINADE FOR CHICKEN

¼ cup olive oil

3 Tbsp. lemon juice

1 tsp. paprika

½ tsp. salt

Makes enough for 2 lbs. chicken breast.
Marinate for 4 - 12 hours.

CHICKEN CACCIATORE

In crock pot, combine all ingredients:

3 lb. boneless, skinless chicken breast
        or 1 large frying chicken, cut up

1 Tbsp. olive oil

1 medium onion, thinly sliced

1 tsp. salt

½ tsp. basil

⅛ tsp. pepper

1 bay leaf

1 quart tomato chunks

1 clove garlic, minced

1 tsp. oregano

½ tsp. celery seed

⅛ tsp. cayenne

Refrigerate and marinade overnight.
Remove from refrigerator next day and cook in marinade on low for
6 - 8 hours, or on high for 3 - 4 hours.
Freeze leftover marinade for blackeye pea soup or chicken chili.
Use in place of juice and broth.
Season to taste.

GOLDEN CHICKEN

(day 1)

In large heavy skillet, combine:
3 Tbsp. olive oil
3 Cornish hens, cut up, or 6 chicken breasts
$1/2$ tsp. salt

Brown on both sides 5 - 10 minutes.
Cover and cook 25 - 30 minutes or until done.
Drain off fat.

Add:
1 large bell pepper, sliced in strips
1 large onion, thinly sliced

Stirring often, continue cooking 5 - 6 minutes or until vegetables are
tender-crisp.   Serves 6

CABBAGE ROLLS

(day 4)

Combine:
1 lb. ground beef or turkey
$1/2$ tsp. ginger
$3/4$ tsp. salt
1 cup cooked brown rice

Boil in water for 5 minutes:
12 cabbage leaves, hard core cut out

Rinse cabbage leaves with cold water.
Divide burger into 12 portions.
Form into flattened balls, and wrap cabbage leaf around each ball.
Place in baking pan in single layer.
Top with ketchup if desired.
Bake uncovered at 350° F. for 1 hour.

FISH FILETS (HAITIAN STYLE)
(day 2)

1 lb. fish filets

We
like to use
Alaskan Pollock
filets. They are
a good tasting
fish, yet are
inexpensive.

Mix:
$1/4$ cup orange juice concentrate
2 Tbsp. water
$1/4$ tsp. nutmeg
$1/4$ tsp. salt

Dip fish into orange juice mixture and place single layer on baking sheet.
Drizzle remaining juice concentrate over fish.
Bake at 375° F. for 30 minutes.
Drain most of juice off to serve.

BAKED FISH
(day 3)

2 lb. fish filets
$1/3$ cup olive oil
2 Tbsp. lemon juice, optional
2 tsp. ginger
$1/8$ tsp. garlic powder, optional
$1/2$ tsp. salt
$1^1/2$ cups quinoa flour, or a mixture of corn and rice flour

Combine dry ingredients.
Dip fish in oil and lemon, then roll in flour.
Arrange in single layer on greased pan.
Bake at 450° F. for 15 - 20 minutes, or until fish flakes easily with fork.

Serves 10

OVEN FRIED FISH
(day 4)

1/3 cup olive oil
1/4 tsp. pepper
1/8 tsp. garlic powder
1 1/2 cups cornmeal or rice flour

2 Tbsp. lemon juice
1/4 tsp. paprika
1 tsp. salt
2 lb. fish filets

Combine oil, lemon juice, and spices.
Dip fish in mixture and roll in flour.
Arrange fish in single layer on greased pan.
Bake at 450° F. for 15 - 20 minutes, or until fish flakes easily with
a fork.   Serves 10

Spiritual Nugget:
Thank God for
what you have.
Trust God for
what you
need.

PARSLEY BREADED FISH

1 lb. fish filets, thawed
1/4 cup olive oil
1 Tbsp. dry parsley flakes
1/2 tsp. salt
1/4 tsp. paprika

1/2 cup dry bread crumbs,
              finely crumbled
1/4 tsp. oregano
1/4 tsp. basil
1/8 tsp. pepper

Mix dry ingredients.
Dip fish in oil, then in crumb mixture.
Bake at 375° F. for 20 - 25 minutes.

SALMON PATTIES
(day 1 use mackerel)

1 - 15 oz. can salmon or mackerel, drained
1/4 cup chopped onions
1/2 cup rolled oats or spelt
1 egg or 1/4 cup water
1/4 tsp. dry mustard
1 Tbsp. olive oil

Combine all ingredients except oil. Add a little more water if too dry
to form patties. Form patties and roll in flour if desired.
Heat oil in heavy skillet over medium heat.
Brown patties on both sides.
Serve immediately.   Serves 4

SALMON PUFFS
(day 4 or 1)

Beat:
1 egg or ¹/₄ cup water

Add:
1 - 15 oz. can salmon or mackerel, drained
¹/₂ cup rolled oats or bread crumbs
1 Tbsp. lemon juice
¹/₄ tsp. pepper, optional

¹/₂ cup water
1 small onion, diced
¹/₄ tsp. salt
1 Tbsp. olive oil

Mix until well blended.
Place in 8 or 9 well greased muffin tins.
Bake at 350° F. for 45 - 50 minutes.

Spiritual Nugget:
Man looks at the outward appearance, but the Lord looks within.

TUNA BROCCOLI LOAF

2 - 6 oz. cans tuna, undrained
1¹/₂ cups chopped fresh or frozen broccoli
1 small onion, chopped
¹/₂ cup meat broth or water
2 slices bread (crumbs)
¹/₄ tsp. salt

Combine all ingredients in a bowl. Place in a greased loaf pan.
If desired, spread ketchup over loaf.
Bake uncovered at 350° F. for 40 - 50 minutes.

SALMON BROCCOLI LOAF - substitute 1 - 15 oz. can salmon instead of tuna. May also substitute mackerel.

TUNA PATTIES
(day 3)

1 - 6 oz. can tuna, drained
2 Tbsp. olive oil
1 Tbsp. chives

2 Tbsp. water
¹/₂ stalk celery, chopped fine
¹/₂ tsp. guar gum

Mix all ingredients.
Shape into patties.
Fry in hot greased skillet.

LENTIL BURGERS

(day 3)

2 cups lentils, well cooked
1 cup water
$\frac{1}{2}$ cup quinoa or kamut flour
1 cup whole grain bread crumbs
1 onion, chopped
$\frac{1}{2}$ cup celery, chopped
1 Tbsp. parsley, chopped
1 tsp. thyme
$\frac{1}{2}$ tsp. sage
1 tsp. salt
4 Tbsp. olive oil

Mix all ingredients together, adding a little water if too thick.
Fry patties in olive oil or bake on greased baking pan at 350° F.
for 20 - 25 minutes.   Yields 3 - 4 servings

Hint:
To make equal sized meatballs, pat meat into a 1 inch thick square. Cut into the same number of equal sized squares as meatballs in the recipe. Roll each square into a ball.

MEATBALLS

1 lb. ground beef or turkey
2 Tbsp. ketchup
$\frac{1}{2}$ cup whole grain bread crumbs
1 small onion, finely chopped
1 carrot, finely grated
$\frac{1}{4}$ tsp. salt
$\frac{1}{8}$ tsp. pepper

Mix all together.
Make about 1$\frac{1}{2}$" meatballs.

Top with:
2 cups tomato chunks or spread ketchup on top.

Bake at 350° F. for 1 hour in uncovered baking dish.
                                    Yields 12 meatballs

STUFFED PEPPERS

(day 1)

Cut in half:

3 large peppers

Remove seeds and pulp. Place in baking dish and fill with meat mixture.

Combine:

1 lb. ground venison or beef
$^1/_2$ cup chopped onion
2 cups pinto or black turtle beans
$1^1/_2$ cups peeled, chopped tomato
$^3/_4$ tsp. salt
$^1/_2$ tsp. oregano

Top with ketchup if desired.   Bake uncovered at 350° F. for $1^1/_2$ hours.

VEGGIE MEAT LOAF

1 cup chicken broth
1 large carrot, finely chopped
1 stalk celery, chopped
1 onion, chopped

Cook vegetables in broth 5 - 10 minutes or until soft.

Meanwhile mix:

1 lb. ground beef or turkey
1 slice bread (crumbs)
$^1/_2$ cup fresh parsley
$^1/_2$ tsp. salt
$^1/_4$ tsp. pepper

Add cooked vegetables and mix.
Place in loaf pan, leaving room along sides for juice and grease to collect. Bake at 350° F. for $1^1/_4$ - $1^1/_2$ hours.

Spiritual Nugget:
The real measure of a man's wealth is what he has invested in eternity.

Soups
and
Sandwiches

*Dorisa wraps the franks in their "blanket" for a
yummy meal of "Dorisa's Pigs in a Blanket."*

ASPARAGUS SOUP

In medium sized kettle, heat:
2 Tbsp. olive oil

Add and saute:
1 stalk celery, chopped
1 medium onion, chopped

Add:
2 cups chicken or turkey broth
1 cup cooked chicken, chopped

Bring to a boil and add:
5 cups fresh or frozen asparagus, thawed

Cover and simmer 4 - 5 minutes until tender-crisp.

Meanwhile, stir:
3 Tbsp. cornstarch or 3 Tbsp. arrowroot starch into 1$\frac{1}{2}$ cups water
(heat until thickened, but do not boil arrowroot)

If using cornstarch, stir into soup and cook 2 minutes, stirring constantly.

Add:
$\frac{3}{4}$ tsp. salt
$\frac{1}{8}$ tsp. nutmeg

Cover and simmer 20 - 25 minutes, stirring occasionally.   Serves 6 - 8

BARLEY CABBAGE SOUP
(day 4)

In a kettle, place:
$\frac{1}{2}$ lb. ground beef, browned
1 cup hulled barley
6 cups water
1 tsp. salt

Bring to a boil and simmer, covered, for $\frac{1}{2}$ hour.

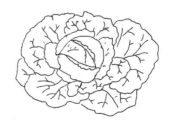

Add over top:
6 cups cabbage, chopped

Do not stir. Cover and simmer $\frac{1}{2}$ hour longer.

Serves 10

BEAN SOUP

(day 1)

5 cups vegetable broth, blended
1¹/₂ cups dry navy beans
1 tsp. salt

Bring to a boil. Cover and simmer 2 hours.   Serves 6 - 8

BLACKEYE PEA SOUP I

(day 3)

3 cups dry blackeye peas
6 cups water

Bring peas and water to a boil. Cook 3 minutes. Turn heat off. Cover and soak 1 hour. Drain.

2 cups broth	1 tsp. ginger
2 cups water	¹/₂ tsp. thyme
2 Tbsp. chives or 1 small onion, minced	³/₄ tsp. salt
1 stalk celery, chopped	dash of pepper
fresh parsley or other chopped greens	

Add broth, water, celery, and onions to peas. Bring to a boil and simmer 20 - 30 minutes. Add seasoning and parsley.   Serves 8 - 10

BLACKEYE PEA SOUP II

(day 3)

4 cups chicken broth or water
4 medium potatoes, diced
1 stalk celery, diced
2 cups blackeye peas or kidney beans, cooked
1 leek, diced
1 clove garlic, minced, optional
1 tsp. salt
¹/₂ tsp. basil
¹/₂ tsp. thyme

Combine all ingredients.
Bring to a boil and simmer 45 minutes to 1 hour.
                              Serves 9

BROCCOLI CHICKEN SOUP

Bring to a boil:
4 cups chicken broth
2 cups cooked chicken, chopped

Add:
1 large bunch broccoli, chopped
1 small onion, chopped
1 stalk celery, chopped

Simmer 15 - 20 minutes.

Add and heat:

1 tsp. lemon juice	2 cups tomato juice
1/2 tsp. salt	1/4 tsp. thyme
dash of pepper	

Spiritual Nugget:
"Endurance" is.... maintaining my commitment to God during times of pressure.

Serves 8

CABBAGE SOUP

(day 4)

1/2 lb. ground beef, browned	1/2 tsp. salt
4 cups meat broth or water	1/8 tsp. allspice
1 head cabbage, chopped	1 Tbsp. lemon
1 onion, chopped	

Simmer meat, broth, cabbage, onion, and salt 45 minutes to 1 hour.
Add allspice and lemon and serve.   Serves 6 - 8

CELERY SOUP

(day 3)
Saute in 2 Tbsp. olive oil:
1/2 cup leeks or onion, diced
2 cups celery, diced

Add:

2 cups chicken broth or water	1 cup potatoes, diced
1/2 tsp. rosemary	1 tsp. salt
1/8 tsp. pepper, optional	

Simmer 20 minutes or until potatoes are soft.   Serves 6

CHICKEN CHILI

4 cups tomato juice
4 cups cooked kidney, black, or pinto beans
2 cups chicken or turkey broth
1 cup cooked chicken, chopped
1 cup carrots, diced
1 tsp. salt
1 tsp. thyme
1 tsp. chili powder, optional

In kettle, bring all ingredients to a boil.
Simmer at least $1/2$ hour on low heat.

Serves 11

CHILI AND BISCUITS

Prepare Chicken Chili or your own favorite chili and top with cornmeal biscuits.

Biscuits:
1 cup rice flour
1 cup cornmeal
2 tsp. baking powder
$1/8$ tsp. salt
$1/2$ tsp. guar gum
1 cup water
1 Tbsp. olive oil

Put 2 quarts hot chili in 9 x 13" pan.
Mix biscuits in order given until just barely mixed.
Drop by spoonfuls onto hot chili.
Bake uncovered at 400° F. for 35 - 40 minutes or until lightly browned.

CHICKEN NOODLE CABBAGE SOUP

Bring to a boil in kettle:
6 cups chicken broth
1½ cups cooked, diced chicken

Add:
4 cups cabbage, chopped

Cover and simmer for ½ hour.

Add:
1 small garlic clove, minced, optional
8 oz. whole grain noodles
1 tsp. ginger
salt to taste

Cover and simmer 20 - 25 minutes.   Serve immediately.

Serves 8

Spiritual Nugget:
Salvation is free, but discipleship is costly.

CHICKEN VEGETABLE SOUP

Bring to a boil and simmer, covered, ½ hour:
1 quart chicken broth or water
1 cup cooked chicken, chopped
1 medium onion, diced
2 carrots, diced

Add:
2 cups chopped cabbage
1 zucchini, quartered lengthwise and then sliced
1 tsp. salt

Simmer 20 - 30 minutes longer.

Serves 8

CREAM OF BEAN SOUP

(day 1)
(Creamy and delicious!)

Saute in 3 Tbsp. olive oil:
1 medium onion, minced
$^1/_2$ cup carrots, finely diced
1 Tbsp. peppers, chopped fine

Puree in blender:
2 cups cooked beans (navy, pinto, or northern)
1$^1/_2$ cups water

Stir into vegetables.

Add:
2 cups cooked beans (same kind as above)
$^3/_4$ tsp. salt

Bring to a boil and simmer, covered, 5 minutes.

Add and serve:
1 Tbsp. parsley   Serves 5

CREAM SOUP   (Substitute for Campbell's Soups)

6 Tbsp. olive oil $^1/_2$ tsp. salt
$^1/_2$ cup spelt flour or $^3/_4$ cup rice flour $^1/_4$ tsp. pepper
1 Tbsp. instant chicken seasoning   4 cups milk or rice milk

In skillet, mix all ingredients except milk. Heat until bubbly. Remove from heat and slowly blend in part of the milk. Return to medium heat and continue stirring in the rest of the milk as it thickens. Boil 1 minute, stirring constantly.

Store in refrigerator up to 1 week, or freeze in 1 - 2 cup containers up to 1 month.
Handy for quick casseroles.

Variations:
   Mushroom Soup - Add 4 oz. can finely chopped mushrooms.
   Celery Soup - Add 1 cup blanched finely diced celery.
   Chicken Soup - Add $^1/_2$ cup finely chopped leftover chicken.

CREAMY GARDEN CHOWDER

In large kettle, combine:

4 cups broth or water
2 cups carrots, chopped
1 cup cauliflower, diced
1 medium onion, chopped
pepper to taste

4 cups potatoes, diced
1 cup celery, diced
2 Tbsp. green pepper, chopped
1 tsp. salt
1 Tbsp. chicken seasoning, optional

Bring to a boil. Cover and simmer 1/2 hour or until vegetables are tender.

Combine:

1 cup rice milk
1/4 cup rice flour

Stir into boiling soup. Stir and continue cooking 2 minutes.
Garnish with parsley.

Serves 11

Spiritual Nugget:

When faith is the most difficult, it is the most necessary.

CREAMY VEGETABLE SOUP

Simmer until just tender, 20 minutes:

3 cups chicken broth
1 1/2 cups carrots, chopped
1 cup broccoli, chopped
1 medium onion, chopped

2 cups cooked chicken, chopped
1 1/2 cups cauliflower, chopped
1/2 cup celery, chopped
1 tsp. salt

Dissolve:

3 Tbsp. cornstarch or arrowroot flour in 1/4 cup water. (Do not cook after adding arrowroot.)

Stir into soup.
Cook 2 minutes, stirring constantly until thickened.

Add:

2 Tbsp. parsley

Serves 10 - 12

CROCK POT VEGETABLE SOUP
(day 1)
Brown in 2 Tbsp. olive oil:
1 lb. venison steak, cut in $1/2$" cubes

Combine in crock pot with meat and broth from browning:

1 quart tomato chunks	1 large onion
3 cups water	$1/2$ tsp. basil
3 carrots, sliced	$3/4$ tsp. salt
$1/2$ tsp. oregano	

Cook on high for 5 hours.

Add:
2 cups cooked black turtle, navy, or pinto beans
2 cups canned green beans

Cook on high for 1 hour or until meat and vegetables are tender.

Serves 8 - 10

FISH CHOWDER

4 Tbsp. olive oil	4 cups water
$1/2$ cup onion, finely chopped	4 cups potatoes, diced
4 Tbsp. spelt flour	2 cups rice milk or broth
$2^1/2$ tsp. salt	2 Tbsp. olive oil
$1/8$ tsp. pepper	2 lb. fish

Heat 4 Tbsp. oil in a large kettle. Saute onions about 5 minutes.
Add **flour, salt,** and **pepper.** Stir. Add water and potatoes. Bring to a
boil; **reduce** heat and simmer 15 - 20 minutes, stirring occasionally.
Meanwhile, cut fish into 1" squares. Cook in 2 Tbsp. oil for 6 minutes,
turning every 2 minutes. Add milk and fish to rest of ingredients.
To serve, sprinkle with parsley, if desired.   Serves 10 -12

Note: For *(day 4)* **FISH CHOWDER:**
Make the following changes to above recipe:
Omit onion.
Use rice flour in place of spelt flour.
3 cups **water** in place of 4 cups water.
3 cups **cooked** rice in place of potatoes

BASIL GREEN BEAN SOUP
(day 1)

Saute in 1 Tbsp. olive oil:
1 cup onion, chopped

Add:
4 cups water
2 cups parsnips or potatoes, diced
1 cup carrots, diced

Simmer, covered, for 20 minutes or until vegetables are soft.

Add:
1 quart green beans
1 tsp. salt
1 tsp. basil

Heat and serve.   Serves 8

HEARTY WHITE BEAN SOUP

Bring to boil in large kettle:
2 cups dry navy beans or other white beans
1 cup brown rice
4 cups chicken broth or water
5 cups water

Cover and simmer $1/2$ hour.

Add:
1 onion, chopped
1 cup carrots, chopped
1 stalk celery, chopped
1 medium zucchini, quartered lengthwise, then sliced thin, optional

Cook $3/4$ - 1 hour longer.

Add and serve:
$1/8$ tsp. pepper, optional
1 tsp. salt
$1/4$ tsp. thyme
fresh parsley, minced for garnish

                                        Serves 12

Forgot to soak your dry beans overnight? Cover the beans with water. Bring to a boil. Remove from heat, and let set for 1 - $1\frac{1}{2}$ hours. Drain soak water, and add fresh water to cover beans. Cook 1 - $1\frac{1}{2}$ hours until soft. Changing the soak water helps to make the beans less gassy.

KALE SOUP

(day 2)

Bring to a boil:
4 cups turkey broth

Add:
2 cups diced, cooked turkey
$1/8$ tsp. pepper
2 bunches kale, stemmed and chopped

Cover and simmer 5 minutes or until kale is soft.

Serves 6

ITALIAN LENTIL SOUP

Bring to a boil:
$3^1/2$ cups broth or water   1 large stalk celery, chopped
$1^1/2$ cups lentils   1 medium onion, chopped
1 bay leaf

Simmer covered for 30 - 40 minutes.

Remove bay leaf and add:
1 cup pizza sauce or water   1 tsp. salt
$1/8$ tsp. pepper, optional $1/2$ tsp. Italian seasoning
5 "Shelton's" chicken franks, sliced, optional

Reheat and serve.

Serves 8

LENTIL RICE SOUP

6 cups meat broth
1 cup brown rice
$1/2$ cup lentils
1 medium onion, chopped
1 clove garlic, minced
$1/2$ tsp. fresh or $1/4$ tsp. dry dill
1 tsp. salt

Bring all ingredients to a boil. Simmer, covered, for 1 hour.
For variety add carrots, zucchini, or parsley.

Serves 8

QUINOA PEA SOUP

(day 3)

3 Tbsp. olive oil
1 cup quinoa
1 stalk celery, diced
1 leek, chopped
4 cups water
2 cups peas
1 tsp. salt
$^1/_2$ tsp. rosemary

In large kettle, heat olive oil.
Saute quinoa, celery, and leek in oil for 3 - 5 minutes.
Add water.
Bring to a boil and simmer, covered, for 10 minutes.
Add peas, salt, and rosemary.
Cook 5 - 10 minutes longer.   Serves 8

SAVORY SUMMER SOUP

2 cups rice
6 cups broth
2 cups chicken, cooked
1 cup carrots, diced
3 cups zucchini, sliced
$1^1/_2$ tsp. salt
$^1/_8$ tsp. pepper

Combine all ingredients in $2^1/_2$ quart casserole.
Bake at 350° F. for $1^1/_2$ hours.

Variation: To cook on top of stove: Bring all ingredients except
zucchini to a boil and simmer 45 minutes.
Add zucchini and simmer 20 minutes longer.

Spiritual
Nugget:
Do I love people
and use things;
(or) Do I love
things and use
people?

SIZZLING RICE SOUP

Press into oiled baking pan, about 1/2" thick:
4 cups cooked rice, cold

Spread olive oil over top.

Bake uncovered at 300° F. for 1 hour.
Cut into 1 1/2" pieces.
Remove from pan, turning pieces over onto cookie sheet.
Bake 1/2 - 1 hour longer or until dry and crisp.

SOUP

Bring to a boil:
6 cups chicken broth
2 cups cooked chicken, chopped

Add:
2 medium carrots, chopped
1 onion, diced
1 1/2 cups cabbage, chopped
1 tsp. salt

Simmer 10 minutes.
To serve, put baked rice cakes in serving bowls and ladle soup over.

Serves 6 - 8

POTATO SOUP

4 cups meat broth
3 carrots, cubed
6 medium potatoes, unpeeled, cubed
1 parsnip, cubed, optional
1 tsp. salt
parsley for garnish

Cook vegetables in broth until tender, 30 - 45 minutes.
Add salt and parsley and serve.

Serves 6 - 8

SWEET POTATO SOUP

4 cups chicken broth
2 cups cooked chicken, chopped
4 cups sweet potatoes, diced
4 cups white potatoes, diced
1 medium onion, diced
$\frac{1}{2}$ tsp. thyme, optional
2 tsp. salt
pepper to taste

Combine all ingredients except seasoning in kettle.
Bring to a boil.
Simmer, covered, about 45 minutes.
Add seasoning and serve.   Serves 10 - 12

TURKEY NOODLE SOUP
                    (day 2)
4 cups turkey broth
4 cups water
1 cup cooked turkey or chicken, chopped
1 tsp. salt
1 lb. spelt noodles

Bring water, broth, turkey, and salt to a boil.
Add noodles and bring to a boil again.
Turn burner off and allow to set, covered, for 25 minutes.
Serve.   Serves 10

*Food
for Thought:
Although the tongue
weighs
very little, few
people are able
to hold
it.*

DANAE'S BROILED
TURKEY & CHEESE SANDWICH

Toast bread.
Spread with mayonnaise.
Cover with thinly sliced cooked turkey or chicken breast, and thin tomato slices.
Top with thin slices of cheese. See Dairy Free Cheese (page 146).
Broil until cheese melts.

Spiritual
Nugget:
Faith is the link
that connects our
weakness to
God's
strength.

DARLA'S SPINACH SANDWICH
(day 2)

1 slice spelt bread
mayonnaise
spinach

Spread mayonnaise on bread.
Pile high with spinach.
Enjoy!

TUNA CRUNCH SANDWICH
(day 3)

1 - 6 oz. can tuna, flaked
$1/4$ cup dill pickles, finely chopped, optional
1 cup shredded lettuce
$1/8$ tsp. salt
$1/3$ cup mayonnaise, or enough to spread easily (page 101)

Spread on kamut bread (page 26) or bread of your choice.

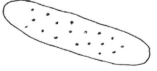

78

CREAMED TURKEY SANDWICH

(day 2)
(Your guests will ask for seconds!)

Saute in 2 Tbsp. olive oil:
2 medium onions, diced
2 stalks celery, diced
1 red or green bell pepper, chopped
 Set aside.

Bring to a boil:
4¹/₂ cups turkey broth

Stir into 1 cup cold water:
1¹/₂ cups spelt flour
4 tsp. salt

Stir into boiling broth.
Process in blender if it gets lumpy.
Bring to a boil again and cook for 2 minutes, stirring constantly.

Place in crock pot:
15 cups cooked turkey, chopped

Stir in vegetables and broth.
Cook on low at least 4 hours or as long as 8 hours,
or bake at 300° F. for 2 hours.
If cold, bake at 350° F for 1¹/₂ hours.

Makes 35 - 40 sandwiches

Hint: Not having guests? Cut recipe in half.
Leftovers can be put in small containers and frozen for future cold or
warmed turkey sandwiches.

*Food
for Thought:*
*A critical spirit
is like poison ivy –
it only takes a
little contact to
spread its
poison.*

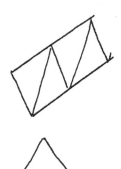

DORISA'S PIGS IN A BLANKET
(day 2)
10 "Sheltons" turkey franks

Mix together:
1 cup spelt flour
1½ tsp. baking powder
¼ tsp. salt
¼ tsp. guar gum
2 Tbsp. olive oil

Stir in:
⅓ cup water

Roll out ⅛" thick on flour covered countertop.
Cut in 4" squares.
Cut each square in half diagonally, forming triangles.
Starting at one of narrow ends of triangle, roll each piece around turkey franks.
Seal end of dough by pinching into roll.
Bake with sealed edge underneath at 450° F. for 20 minutes.

Yields 10 franks

PEPPER VENISON SANDWICH
(day 1)
Saute in 2 Tbsp. olive oil:
1 bell pepper, diced
1 large onion, thinly sliced

In a separate skillet, brown:
1 lb. ground venison

Stir 2 Tbsp. arrowroot starch or cornstarch into ¾ cup water.
Stir into meat and bring to a boil and cook 1 minute. (Do not boil arrowroot.)

Add:
sauteed vegetables
½ tsp. salt

Serve on bread or buns.

Food for Thought:
Happy memories never wear out.... relive them as often as you wish.

Vegetables

Mary is training her "Prizetaker" limas.
She likes to grow her own produce -
assuring fresh and wholesome quality.

ORANGE ASPARAGUS
(day 2)

2 lb. asparagus, cut in 1" pieces
2 oranges
$1/2$ tsp. ginger

1 Tbsp. lemon juice
$1/2$ tsp. salt

Cook the asparagus in a small amount of water for 3 - 4 minutes, or until tender-crisp.
Add peeled and halved oranges, slice cross ways, making small pieces. Pull sections apart.
Add lemon juice, ginger, and salt.
Heat 1 minute and serve.

BRUSSELS SPROUTS

Cook in a small amount of water for 15 minutes:
2 cups brussels sprouts

Drain.

Saute in 1 Tbsp. olive oil:
1 small clove garlic, minced

Add:
brussels sprouts
1 tsp. lemon juice

Simmer, covered, 5 - 10 minutes.

Add:
1 tsp. parsley
$1/4$ tsp. salt
dash pepper

*Food
for Thought:
To be angry with
a weak man is
proof that we are
not very strong
ourselves.*

CAULI-TATERS

2 Tbsp. olive oil in skillet
1 cup cauliflower florets
3 cups cooked potatoes, sliced
salt and pepper to taste

Cook covered until cauliflower is just soft.
Serve immediately.

Serves 6

SAUTEED EGGPLANT
(day 3)

3 Tbsp. olive oil
1 medium eggplant, peeled and diced
1 clove garlic, minced
$1/4$ tsp. salt
$1/2$ tsp. curry powder

Heat heavy skillet.
Add olive oil and garlic. Saute 1 - 2 minutes over low heat.
Turn heat to medium and add eggplant.
Turn constantly for 5 - 10 minutes or until browned and soft, but not mushy. Add seasonings and serve immediately.

Serves 4 - 6

EGGPLANT PATTIES
(day 3)

Bring to a boil:
1 large eggplant, peeled and cut in chunks
$1/2$ cup water

Simmer, covered, for 20 minutes or until tender.
Drain well and mash.

Add:
$3/4$ cup quinoa flour
$1/2$ tsp. salt
1 Tbsp. chives, chopped
$1/8$ tsp. pepper, optional

When cool enough to handle, shape into patties, and cook until browned in heated skillet with olive oil.

Serves 3 - 4

ELEGANT GREEN BEANS
(day 3)

Heat:
1 quart canned green beans
salt to taste

Add and stir together:
$1/4$ cup slivered almonds

Serve.

GARLIC MASHED POTATOES

8 medium potatoes
3 cloves garlic, finely minced
1 cup rice milk

1 Tbsp. olive oil
1 tsp. salt
$\frac{1}{8}$ tsp. pepper

Peel and cut potatoes in chunks. Cook potatoes in 1 to 2" of water until tender.
Meanwhile brown garlic in olive oil. Set aside.
Whip potatoes with cooking water until smooth. Add salt, pepper and garlic.
Beat on low speed while slowly adding milk until desired consistency.
Serve with gravy or noodles cooked in meat broth.

BAKED POTATO CHIPS

(day 3)

3 baking potatoes, unpeeled
3 Tbsp. olive oil
$\frac{1}{2}$ tsp. salt
$\frac{1}{2}$ tsp. rosemary

Slice potatoes $\frac{1}{8}$" or thinner.
Stir salt and rosemary into oil.
Toss potatoes and oil mixture together until well coated. Place in single layer on cookie sheet.
Bake at 425° F. for 15 minutes.
Turn and bake an additional 5 minutes or until brown and crisp.

Serves 3 - 4

> **Tip:**
> **For dairy free mashed potatoes:**
> Mashed potatoes with olive oil added in place of butter have a delicious, rich flavor, not otherwise possible without the addition of butter. Use about half the amount you would of butter.

GOLDEN BAKED POTATOES

(day 3)

Roll potatoes with peels on in olive oil and place in baking pan.
Cover loosely with foil.

For variety add a little garlic powder or garlic salt to the olive oil.

Bake at 400° F. for 1 hour or until tender.

FINGER LICKIN' GOOD POTATOES
(day 3)

6 medium unpeeled baking potatoes, sliced 1/8" thick
1/4 cup olive or canola oil
1/2 cup quinoa, rice, or spelt flour
paprika, garlic powder, salt, and pepper to taste

Pour oil over potatoes.
Cover and shake to coat potatoes.
Sprinkle flour and seasoning mixture over potatoes and shake again.
Place potatoes in single layer on greased pan.
Bake at 450° F. for 20 minutes or until potatoes are done.

Serves 8

CHIVE POTATOES
(day 3)

5 medium potatoes, cut in 1/2" cubes

Mix:
1/4 cup olive oil
2 Tbsp. chives, cut in 1/4" pieces
3/4 tsp. salt

Toss potatoes with chive mixture.
Bake covered at 400° F. for 35 minutes.
Uncover and bake 15 minutes longer.

Serves 6 - 8

CRISPY POTATO WEDGES
(day 3)

6 potatoes
1/4 cup olive oil
3/4 tsp. salt
1/8 tsp. garlic powder

3/4 cup quinoa flour
1 1/2 tsp. paprika
1/8 tsp. pepper

Cut potatoes in half. Cut each half in thirds or fourths.
In covered container, shake potatoes and oil together.
Combine the rest of the ingredients in a covered container.
Shake 5 or 6 potatoes at a time in flour mixture.
Place potatoes in a single layer on greased cookie sheet.
Bake at 375° F. for 1 hour, or at 400° F for 1/2 hour.

LUO POTATOES (KENYA)

Heat in skillet:
3 Tbsp. olive oil

Add and saute:
1 medium onion, minced   1 tomato, chunked

Add:
6 medium potatoes, diced $^3/_4$"
$^1/_4$ cup water $^1/_2$ tsp. salt

Cover and cook on medium-low heat until done, about 20 minutes.
Serves 6 - 8

The
best
potatoes
come to
the table
with their
jackets
on.

OVEN FRENCH FRIES

(day 3)
3 medium potatoes $^1/_4$ cup olive oil
salt

Cut potatoes in $^3/_8$" slices, then into $^3/_8$" sticks.
In a tightly sealed container, shake potatoes and oil to coat evenly.
Spread out on single layer on cookie sheet.
Bake at 450° F. for 30 - 40 minutes.
Drain on crumpled paper towel.
Sprinkle with salt.

SCALLOPED POTATOES

Simmer, covered, 20 minutes in skillet:
$^1/_2$ cup water   1 large sweet onion, sliced
1 clove garlic or $^1/_8$ tsp. garlic powder   dash of black pepper
$^3/_4$ tsp. salt

Meanwhile thinly slice:
6 potatoes

Liquefy ingredients from skillet in blender.
Stir into potatoes.
Pour back into skillet and simmer $^1/_2$ hour or until tender,
or place in casserole and bake covered at 350° F. for 50 - 60 minutes.
Serves 8 - 10

STUFFED BAKED POTATOES

Bake uncovered until well done, 4 large potatoes

Meanwhile combine:

1 - 6 oz. can tuna	¹/₄ tsp. salt
1 cup cream soup (page 70)	¹/₂ cup blanched peas
2 Tbsp. snipped chives	¹/₄ cup green peppers, diced
¹/₂ cup grated "Dairy Free Cheese" (page 146)	

Cut potatoes in half lengthwise. Take potato pulp out without breaking the skin. Mash the pulp and fold in the sauce mixture. Heap mixture into the potato shells. Bake at 400° F. for 15 - 20 minutes or until browned.

SAUTEED SPINACH

(day 2)

3 Tbsp. olive oil
1 lb. spinach, chopped
¹/₄ tsp. salt

Heat oil in large, heavy skillet.
Add spinach and saute 3 - 5 minutes, stirring constantly.
Add salt and serve.

Serves 6 - 8

BAKED SWEET POTATO DELUXE

Combine in casserole:
4 cups sweet potatoes, unpeeled, diced
1 apple, sliced
¹/₂ tsp. salt
¹/₃ cup raisins
¹/₄ cup coconut
¹/₄ cup water

Bake covered at 375° F. for 1 hour or until potatoes are soft.

Sprinkle over top to serve:
¹/₂ cup walnuts or pecans, chopped

OVEN FRIED WINTER SQUASH

Slice in 1/8 - 1/4" slices:
1 butternut or other winter squash

Dip in olive oil and place in cake pan.

Sprinkle with:
salt   basil
garlic powder   parsley flakes

Bake uncovered at 425° F. for 15 - 20 minutes.

PEAS AND BABY POTATOES
(day 3)

Cook covered in a little water until tender:
1 lb. small early potatoes

Saute in 2 Tbsp. olive oil:
1 leek, thinly sliced, or 1 Tbsp. snipped chives

Add:
2 cups peas, blanched
potatoes
1/2 tsp. salt

Heat and serve.

Serves 8

ROASTED SUCCOTASH

2 cups corn   1 small onion, minced
1 cup limas   2 Tbsp. red bell pepper
1 Tbsp. olive oil   1 tsp. cumin
1/4 tsp. salt

Combine all ingredients.
Spread out in 9 x 13" pan.
Bake at 400° F. for 25 minutes or until lightly browned.
Stir when half done.

Butternut squash can be used in place of pumpkin in pumpkin recipes.

MASHED VEGETABLES

1 cup peeled turnips, chopped
1 1/2 cups carrots, chopped
1 cup peeled sweet potatoes, chopped
1/2 tsp. salt
1/8 tsp. pepper, optional

In a medium saucepan combine the turnips, carrots, and sweet potatoes, and 1 inch of water or enough to cook vegetables.
Bring to a boil.
Lower heat and cook about 30 minutes or until very soft.
Add salt and pepper.
Mash vegetables in a mixing bowl.
Add cashew, soy, or rice milk if too stiff.   Serves 4 - 6

STEAMED VEGETABLES

In a large kettle bring about 1" of water to a boil.
Place metal colander with vegetables, cut in bite size pieces into kettle.
Keep vegetables above the water.
Cover. Keep water boiling rapidly.

Asparagus	5 minutes	Carrots	5-6 minutes
Broccoli	4 minutes	Cauliflower	5 minutes
Cabbage	5 minutes		

Check vegetables and steam a little longer if needed. They should be tender-crisp. Serve immediately.

ZUCCHINI PATTIES

2 cups grated zucchini
2 eggs, beaten, or 1/4 cup water
2 Tbsp. olive oil

1 cup brown rice or spelt flour
1/8 tsp. pepper
1 tsp. baking powder
1/8 tsp. salt

Mix first 3 ingredients together.
Mix dry ingredients and add to zucchini.
Drop by spoonfuls onto hot greased skillet
(butter works best if omitting eggs).
Fry until brown on both sides.
Delicious plain, or with tomato slice.

Salads

Nutritious salads can be made up from a large variety of fresh healthy produce.

CITRUS APPLE SALAD

(day 2)

2 large Yellow Delicious, unpeeled apples, chopped
1 large Red Delicious, unpeeled apple, chopped
1 orange, sectioned and cut in pieces
1 cup pineapple chunks
$1/2$ cup pecans, chopped

Squeeze juice from a lemon over apples to keep them from turning brown.
Toss until well coated.
Add rest of ingredients and toss.

Serves 8

Food for Thought:
Brighten the corner where you are...It may brighten the whole room.

FRESH FRUIT SALAD (Makes 1 gallon)

DRESSING:
Cook together:
3 cups pineapple juice
6 Tbsp. cornstarch
$1/8$ tsp. salt

2 Tbsp. pineapple juice concentrate
2 Tbsp. white grape juice concentrate

Stir constantly until thick.
Cool.

Combine:
2 cups red seedless grapes, halved
2 cups white seedless grapes, halved
4 cups sweet yellow apples, unpeeled, diced
1 cup red apples, unpeeled, diced
1 can pineapple chunks, drained
2 cups oranges, diced
3 large bananas, sliced
$1/2$ cup sliced strawberries or red raspberries for color

Stir dressing into fruit.

PEACH RASPBERRY JELLO SALAD

First layer:

Dissolve:
2 Tbsp. unflavored gelatin or
                    1 large box orange sugar free Jello in:
1/2 cup cold water

Bring to a boil:
1 1/2 cup water

Stir in gelatin.

Add:
1 cup orange juice
1 Tbsp. liquid stevia
2 cups sliced peaches, canned or fresh

Pour into clear 3 quart bowl.
Chill until firm.

Second layer:

Dissolve:
2 Tbsp. unflavored gelatin or
                    1 large box strawberry sugar free Jello in:
1/2 cup cold water

Bring to a boil:
2 1/2 cups apple juice

Stir in gelatin.

Add:
1 Tbsp liquid stevia

Chill until partly set.

Add:
2 cups fresh or frozen raspberries

Carefully spoon over first layer.
Chill until set.

Yields 12 - 14 servings

ALL-IN-ONE SALAD

(day 3)

1 medium head romaine or green leaf lettuce
1 cup frozen or fresh blanched peas
1 leek, minced
1/2 cup cold, cooked chicken, chopped
1 small red beet, shredded

Combine all ingredients.
Serve with your favorite dressing.

BROCCOLI SPINACH SALAD

(day 2)

1/4 lb. spinach leaves, bite size
1 cup broccoli, chopped
2 leaves kale, chopped

Combine and serve with Creamy Avocado Dressing (page 101)
or your favorite dressing.
Sprinkle with sunflower or sesame seeds.

SWEET AND SOUR BROCCOLI
CAULIFLOWER SALAD

(day 2)

Place in salad bowl:
1 bunch broccoli, cut into small florets
small head cauliflower, cut into small florets

DRESSING:

1 Tbsp. apple juice concentrate
1 Tbsp. lemon juice
1 Tbsp. olive oil
1 tsp. salt
1/4 tsp. stevia extract

Combine vegetables and dressing.
Chill 3 hours or overnight.
Stir before serving.

Serves 4 - 6

CABBAGE SLAW

6 cups cabbage, chopped
1 carrot, finely grated
1 stalk celery, chopped

DRESSING:

2 Tbsp. apple juice concentrate
3 Tbsp. vinegar or lemon juice
2 Tbsp. olive oil
1 tsp. salt
1 tsp. stevia
1/2 tsp. dry mustard

Combine dressing ingredients and mix with vegetables.
Refrigerate 8 hours or overnight.

Serves 12

Cool cucumbers! Cucumbers are best if picked in the morning while it is cool. If picking after it is warm, submerge in ice water or refrigerate immediately.

CUCUMBER SALAD
(day 1)
Place in salad bowl:
3 medium cucumbers, thinly sliced
1 small onion, minced or thinly sliced

DRESSING:

1/2 tsp. dry mustard
1/4 tsp. stevia
2 Tbsp. white vinegar

1/2 tsp. celery seed, optional
1/2 tsp. salt
1 Tbsp. water

Combine dressing ingredients.
Add to vegetables and refrigerate overnight to mingle flavors.

4 BEAN SALAD

(day 1)

Combine:

1 cup cooked navy beans
2 cups canned french cut green beans
1/4 cup green pepper, chopped

1 cup cooked pinto beans
1 cup canned yellow beans
1/4 cup onion, minced

DRESSING:

1/3 cup olive oil
1 tsp. stevia

3 Tbsp. vinegar
1/2 tsp. salt

Mix dressing and stir into beans.
Cover and refrigerate until ready to serve.

Food for Thought:
You can't change the past, but you can ruin the present by worrying about the future.

ORANGE CAULIFLOWER SALAD

(day 2)

4 oranges, sliced and sectioned
1 1/2 cups cauliflower, chopped
4 cups spinach leaves, torn

Gently toss ingredients together.

DRESSING:

juice drained from oranges
1/4 tsp. salt
1/8 tsp. paprika

1 Tbsp. lemon juice
2 Tbsp. olive oil

Mix dressing and add to salad.

TROPICAL TURKEY SALAD

(day 2)

1 medium head romaine, red, or green leaf lettuce
1 cup cooked, chopped turkey
1 cup chunk pineapple
1 orange, sectioned and cut in pieces

Serve with mayonaise (page 101).

POTATO SALAD

(day 3)

8 medium cooked potatoes, shredded or diced
4 hard-boiled eggs, diced, optional
$1/2$ cup celery, chopped
1 Tbsp. leeks, chives, or onion, chopped
2 sprigs parsley, chopped fine, optional
salt to taste
paprika

Combine all ingredients gently.
Stir sugar free mayonnaise or cooked dressing into potatoes. Add water if too thick. Refrigerate at least 1 hour before serving.

COOKED DRESSING

2 rounded Tbsp. kamut or spelt flour
$1/2$ tsp. salt
$1/2$ tsp. dry mustard
$1/4$ tsp. stevia
dash of cayenne pepper
1 egg, beaten, or 1 Tbsp. oil + 1 rounded Tbsp. flour
2 Tbsp. olive oil
$3/4$ cup water
$1/4$ cup white vinegar or lemon juice

Combine dry ingredients in saucepan.
Turn heat to medium.
Slowly add liquid ingredients while stirring.
Heat, stirring continuously, until thick and bubbly.
Cool.

SPINACH APPLE SALAD

(day 2)

$1/2$ lb. spinach, chopped
1 Yellow Delicious apple, chopped
sunflower seeds

Dressing:

3 Tbsp. olive oil
1 Tbsp. lemon juice
$1/4$ tsp. salt
$1/4$ tsp. stevia

Toss spinach and apples with dressing.
Sprinkle with sunflower seeds.

Serves 8

SPINACH TURKEY SALAD

(day 2)

$1/2$ lb. spinach
$1/2$ cup cooked turkey, chopped
1 orange, sectioned and cut in pieces
slivered almonds

Toss all ingredients together except almonds.
Sprinkle almonds over top.
Serve with Tangy Dressing (page 102) or your favorite dressing.

SWEET POTATO ALMOND SALAD

(day 2)

$1/4$ lb. spinach
1 cup grated sweet potatoes
1 cup cauliflower florets
$1/4$ cup slivered almonds

Toss ingredients together.
Serve with Tangy Dressing (page 102)
or Creamy Avacado Dressing (page 101).

Spiritual Nugget:
The encouraging words, "Do Not Fear" are found 366 times in the Bible. Once for each day, even when it's leap year!

TABOULI

$1/2$ cup raw bulgur wheat
3 medium tomatoes, chopped
1 cup fresh parsley, chopped
$1/3$ cup diced scallions or onions
$1/2$ cup lemon juice or $1/4$ cup white vinegar
$1/2$ cup olive oil
2 Tbsp. mint, finely chopped, optional
1 tsp. salt
dash of cayenne

Combine all ingredients. Marinate 6 hours.
Serve on a thick bed of lettuce.

Note: For more variety try cooked barley, garbanzo beans, millet, or quinoa in place of bulgur.   Serves 3 - 4

TOSSED SALAD
(day 3)

Toss together in bowl:
1 medium head leaf lettuce
1 stalk celery, chopped
1 Tbsp. chives or leeks, chopped
$1/2$ cup garbanzo beans
$1/2$ cup peas, blanched

Quantities of ingredients may be varied according to taste.
Serve with Celery Seed Dressing (page 101) or your favorite dressing.

Sprinkle over top with:
Popped Quinoa Grains (page 104)

TUNA SALAD
(day 3)

1 medium head leaf lettuce
1 - 6 oz. can tuna, drained
1 stalk celery, chopped
1 Tbsp. chives, snipped in $1/2$" pieces

Serve with Celery Seed Dressing (page 101) or your favorite dressing.

Tip:
Be sure to buy tuna that does not contain vegetable broth as it may contain MSG. One brand that can be bought in the grocery store is "Star Kist" Gourmet Choice. Be sure it contains only tuna with water or olive oil and salt. There is also some available without salt. Other brands are also available in health food stores.

BLENDER MAYONNAISE

In blender:
1 egg or $1/4$ cup tofu
$1/2$ tsp. paprika
2 Tbsp. lemon juice

$1/2$ tsp. dry mustard
$1/2$ tsp. salt
$1/4$ tsp. stevia

Pour in very slowly while blending:
1 cup olive oil

Note: Egg or tofu may be omitted, but it separates.

Delicious! Mix "Blender Mayonnaise" and "French Dressing" together.

CREAMY AVOCADO DRESSING

1 cup avocado, approx.
$3/4$ tsp. salt
$1/2$ tsp. paprika, optional

2 Tbsp. lemon juice
$1/2$ tsp. celery seed
1 cup olive oil

Mix all ingredients except oil in blender until smooth.
Slowly pour in oil while whizzing. Refrigerate.

CELERY SEED DRESSING

Combine in blender:
6 oz. tofu, drained
1 small garlic clove
$1/2$ tsp. dry mustard
2 tsp. celery seed

3 Tbsp. lemon juice
1 Tbsp. onion
$1/4$ tsp. salt
$1/2$ tsp. stevia

While blending, slowly add:
1 cup olive oil

For variety, substitute celery seed with Mrs. Dash, or 1 tsp. marjoram and 2 tsp. paprika. Shake well before serving.

FRENCH DRESSING

1 small onion
1 Tbsp. apple juice concentrate, optional
$1/2$ cup olive oil
$1/4$ cup sugar free ketchup or tomato paste

1 Tbsp. lemon juice
$1/2$ tsp. stevia
$1/2$ tsp. paprika
1 tsp. salt

Blend all ingredients except oil. Slowly pour oil in while blending. Chill. Shake well before serving.

ITALIAN DRESSING I

3 Tbsp. vinegar or lemon juice
1 Tbsp. lemon juice
$1/8$ tsp. garlic powder
$1/8$ tsp. stevia
$1/4$ tsp. celery seed
1 cup olive oil

1 Tbsp. parsley, chopped
1 Tbsp. onion, chopped
$1/2$ tsp. mustard
$1/2$ tsp. salt
dash of black pepper

Combine all ingredients in blender except oil.
While blending, slowly add oil.
Shake well before serving.

ITALIAN DRESSING II

3 Tbsp. lemon juice
1 tsp. dry mustard
$1/4$ tsp. basil
$1/4$ tsp. celery seed
$1^1/3$ cups olive oil

1 dash of garlic powder
$1/2$ tsp. salt
$1/4$ tsp. oregano
$1/2$ tsp. stevia

Combine all ingredients except oil in blender.
Blend on medium speed.
Slowly pour oil in while blending.
Chill.

TANGY DRESSING

1 Tbsp. orange juice concentrate
1 Tbsp. lemon juice
1 Tbsp. chopped onion
1 Tbsp. finely chopped parsley
$1/2$ tsp. salt
$1/4$ tsp. paprika
1 tsp. soy sauce, optional
$1/4$ tsp. dry mustard
$1/2$ cup olive oil

Blend ingredients and chill.
Shake thoroughly before serving.

THOUSAND ISLAND DRESSING
(day 1)

1 cup blender mayonnaise (page 101)
1/4 cup salsa
1 Tbsp. onion, finely chopped

2 Tbsp. relish
1/4 tsp. paprika

Stir together.

VINEGAR AND OIL DRESSING

Combine in pint jar:
1 cup olive oil
1/8 tsp. garlic powder
1/2 tsp. paprika

1/4 cup white vinegar
3/4 tsp. salt

Put lid on and shake.
Can be stored at room temperature.
Shake just before serving.

CROUTONS I

Heat in large skillet:
1/4 cup olive oil

Add:
1/4 tsp. garlic powder
4 cups bread cubes

Turn bread cubes until brown all over.

Add:
1/2 tsp. parsley
1/8 tsp. sage

1/2 tsp. thyme
1/8 tsp. salt

Continue to cook and turn for 1 minute longer.
Be sure cubes are thoroughly dry.
Bake at 250° F. on a shallow pan until dry, if necessary.

Note:
Can be stored at room temperature in a covered container for 4 days.

CROUTONS II

Toast and cut in $\frac{1}{2}$**" cubes:**
5 firm bread slices

Combine:
$\frac{1}{4}$ tsp. garlic powder
$\frac{1}{8}$ tsp. salt
$\frac{1}{4}$ tsp. celery seed
$\frac{1}{8}$ tsp. paprika
$\frac{1}{4}$ cup olive oil

Mix and toss with toasted bread cubes.
Bake at 300° F. for $1\frac{1}{2}$ hours, stirring every half hour.
Cool.

Food for Thought:
Love is strength-
ened by working
through conflicts
together.

POPPED GRAINS

(day 1 or 3)
Sprinkle over salads for a delicious taste treat!

Heat in heavy saucepan on medium-high:
1 Tbsp. olive oil

When oil is hot, add:
2 Tbsp. amaranth or quinoa

Test oil **for** right temperature by dropping several grains into hot oil.
When the grains immediately start sizzling, oil is the right **tempera-**
ture.
If the grains don't sizzle the first try, add **several** more after the oil is
hotter.
When they sizzle, reduce heat to medium, and add the rest of the grain.
Cover and shake to spread grain evenly.
Some of the grain will pop, but most of it will not.
If temperature is just right, the unpopped grain will be toasted a light
brown. If it toasts before it starts popping, the oil is too hot.

Drain on **several** layers of paper towels.

Cakes
and
Cupcakes

100%
Whole
Grain

Whole grains produce delicious, full-bodied, nutritious baked goods!

Tips for
Whole Grain Baking

If your family is hesitant to try these new grains, try using part white and part whole grain. Gradually use less white and more whole grain flours.

Whole grain flours have a short shelf life. They gradually lose nutritional value from the time they are ground. Keep them refrigerated or frozen. If you lack space, they can be left at room temperature for up to a month without danger of becoming rancid.

For bread, flour must be brought to room temperature. In other recipes it is best, but it is not a must.

For really fresh flour, consider making your own as you need it. The "dry" pitcher of the **Vita-Mix** can be used for any grains, or invest in a grain mill such as the **Whisper Mill.** (Check **"Resources"** section in back of book.) Small grains such as millet, quinoa, and amaranth can be ground in your blender at high speed.

Sugar free, whole grain baked goods tend to be rather heavy. Be sure to have oven preheated and pans ready to put batter in. Mix batter quickly and put in oven immediately. After a while you will prefer the heavier full-bodied nutritious baked goods, rather than the light, sweet refined foods.

Guar gum helps baked goods to rise more, and makes them less crumbly. It works best to add guar gum with the dry ingredients rather than the wet.

Sugar free, whole grain baked items need to be refrigerated because they tend to spoil more quickly; however, granola and crackers can be left at room temperature.

ANGEL FOOD CAKE

Rinse a large mixing bowl with warm water and dry very thoroughly.

Beat until frothy:
1³/₄ cups egg whites (12 large), room temperature

Add:
¹/₂ tsp. salt
2 tsp. cream of tartar
1 tsp. stevia

Continue to beat just until whites are smooth, shiny, and stiff, but not dry.

Add:
1 tsp. almond extract
1 tsp. vanilla

Sprinkle by tablespoonfuls over egg whites, using a spatula to fold in just until mixed:
1 cup spelt flour (room temperature)

Spoon batter into ungreased tube pan, rinsed with water.
Bake at 325° F. for 1¹/₄ hours.
Invert pan until cool.

Tip for Mom's little helpers: Children can separate eggs. Have them break eggs open, one at a time, into a funnel placed over a cup. The white will pass through into the cup. Dump the yolk out of the funnel into another container.

AMARANTH CARROT CAKE

(day 1)
Mix together in mixing bowl:

³/₄ cup olive oil
¹/₂ cup raisins
3 cups carrots, grated

1¹/₃ cups banana or applesauce
1 cup chopped nuts

Add:

3 cups amaranth or oat flour
2 tsp. guar gum
1¹/₂ tsp. cinnamon
¹/₂ tsp. nutmeg
¹/₄ tsp. ginger

1 Tbsp. baking powder
1 tsp. soda
1 tsp. salt
1 tsp. stevia

Mix together. Bake in greased 8 x 12" pan at 400° F. for 1 hour.

APPLE CAKE

(day 2)

Beat:
1/2 cup olive oil
1 1/2 cups applesauce
1 egg or 1/2 tsp. guar gum + 1/4 cup water

Add and mix until just moistened:

1 3/4 cups spelt flour	1/2 tsp. baking soda
1/2 tsp. salt	1/2 tsp. baking powder
1/4 tsp. cloves	

Stir in:
1 1/2 cups chopped apples
1/2 cup chopped walnuts or pecans

Pour into 8 inch square greased pan.
Sprinkle 1/2 tsp. cinnamon over top.
Bake at 350° F. for 40 - 45 minutes.

BANANA CAKE

(day 1 use oat flour)

Mix:
1/4 cup olive oil
1 cup mashed banana

Add:
2 1/2 cups spelt or oat flour
1/2 tsp. salt
2 tsp. baking powder

Mix well.
Pour into 8 inch square greased pan.
Bake at 350° F. for 30 - 35 minutes.
Serve with rice milk or fruit.

BLUEBERRY PEACH COBBLER

In 9 x 13" pan, place:
4 cups sliced peaches
2 cups blueberries
$^1/_2$ tsp. cinnamon sprinkled over fruit

BATTER:

Beat:
$^1/_2$ cup olive oil
2 eggs or 2 tsp. guar gum + $^1/_2$ cup water
1 tsp. vanilla

Add:

3 cups spelt, millet, or rice flour
4 tsp. baking powder
1 tsp. salt
1 cup fruit juice or water

1 tsp. stevia
1 tsp. cream of tartar
1 tsp. cinnamon

Mix until just combined.
Pour over fruit.
Bake at 375° F. for 25 - 30 minutes.

MILLET RICE CAKE
(day 4)

When substituting guar gum for eggs it works best to add guar gum with dry ingredients rather than wet.

Beat:
1 cup olive oil
3 eggs or 1 tsp. guar gum + $^1/_2$ cup water
1$^1/_4$ cups juice or water

Add:

2 cups millet flour
1$^1/_2$ cups rice flour
2 tsp. vanilla
1 tsp. soda

1 tsp. cream of tartar
1 tsp. salt
1 tsp baking powder
$^1/_2$ tsp. stevia

Mix until just combined.
Place in greased 8 x 12" pan.
Bake at 350° F. for 40 minutes.
Serve with rice milk, fruit, or juice.

OATMEAL CAKE

(day 1)   *(use oat flour for day 1)*

Beat:

3 bananas	1 cup water
3/4 cup olive oil	2 tsp. vanilla

Add:

3 cups spelt, kamut, or oat flour	2 tsp. cinnamon
2 tsp. soda	1 tsp. stevia
1 tsp. baking powder	1 tsp. salt
1 1/2 cups rolled oats or spelt	

Beat just until mixed. Pour into greased 8 x 12" pan.
Bake at 350° F. for 40 minutes.

Variation: Add 1 1/4 cups almond pulp from making almond milk.
Bake in 9 x 13" pan.

*Food
for Thought:
Love...and you
shall be loved!*

PEACH COBBLER

Place in 8 x 12" pan:
6 cups fresh or canned peaches, chunked

Sprinkle over peaches:
2 tsp. cinnamon

TOPPING:

Place in mixer bowl:
1 cup apple juice or water
1/2 cup olive oil
3/4 cup applesauce
2 tsp. vanilla

Combine:

2 cups rice or millet flour	4 tsp. baking powder
1/2 tsp. cream of tartar	1 tsp. stevia

Add to wet ingredients and mix until just combined.
Pour over peaches.
Bake at 350° F. for 45 - 50 minutes.

Note:
Also good with blackberries or raspberries in place of peaches.

PRUNE CAKE

Beat:
3 eggs or 1 tsp. guar gum + $1/2$ cup water
1 cup olive oil
2 cups shredded, peeled apples

Add and combine:
3 cups spelt flour
$1^1/2$ tsp. stevia
2 tsp. soda
1 tsp. salt
1 tsp. cinnamon
$1/2$ tsp. cloves

Stir in:
2 cups dried prunes, chopped
1 cup chopped nuts

Place in greased tube pan.
Bake at 325° F. for 1 hour and 25 minutes.

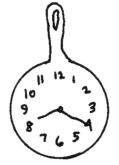

QUINOA CAROB CAKE
(day 3)

Mix:
$3/4$ cup olive oil
$1^1/2$ cups water or apple juice

Add:
$2^1/4$ cups quinoa or amaranth flour
$1/2$ cup carob powder
1 tsp. stevia
$1/2$ tsp. cream of tartar
1 tsp. soda
1 tsp. salt
$1^1/2$ tsp. guar gum

Mix until just combined.
Pour into greased 8 inch square pan.
Bake at 350° F. for 40 minutes.

BLUEBERRY TEA CAKE

(day 3)

Mix together:
1/2 cup olive oil
2 eggs or 1 tsp. guar gum + 1/4 cup water
1 cup water
2 cups kamut or spelt flour
1 Tbsp. baking powder
1 1/2 tsp. stevia
3 cups fresh or frozen blueberries, thawed

Pour batter into greased 9 x 13" pan.

TOPPING:

1/4 cup olive oil
1 tsp. cinnamon
1/2 tsp. allspice

1 cup kamut or spelt flour
1 tsp. nutmeg
1/2 tsp. stevia

Mix and crumble over top of batter.
Bake at 375° F. for 40 - 45 minutes.

ZUCCHINI CARROT CAKE

1/2 cup apple juice or water
1 cup olive oil
2 1/2 cups spelt or oat flour
1 Tbsp. baking powder
1 tsp. soda
2 tsp. stevia
2 tsp. cinnamon

1/2 tsp. ginger
1/2 tsp. allspice
1/2 tsp. nutmeg
1 tsp. salt
2 cups grated zucchini
2 cups grated carrots
1 cup chopped nuts

Combine all ingredients except zucchini, carrots, and nuts.
Fold in last 3 ingredients.
Pour into a greased 8 x 12" baking pan.
Bake at 350° F. for 1 hour.

Tip:
Instead of greasing your cake pans, line the bottom of the pan with waxed paper- cut to fit.

CAROB CUPCAKES

(day 3)

Beat:
$1/2$ cup olive oil
$1/2$ cup carob powder
2 eggs or 1 tsp. guar gum + $1/4$ cup water
1 cup apple juice or water
1 tsp. vanilla

Add:
$2^1/2$ cups kamut or quinoa flour
1 tsp. baking powder
1 tsp. soda
$1/2$ tsp. salt
$1^1/2$ tsp. stevia
$1/2$ cup chopped nuts

Fill cake cups $2/3$ full.
Bake at 350° F. for 30 - 35 minutes.

Yields 18 cupcakes

Tip:
Whole grain, sugar free muffins and cupcakes tend to stick to the bottom of paper liners. Try using foil liners or grease the muffin tin and don't use liners.

CAROB DATE ICING

Combine in saucepan:
$1/4$ cup date pieces
$1/2$ cup carob powder
$3/4$ cup water

Cook until thick and smooth.

Add:
$1/2$ tsp. vanilla

Spread onto cake while hot.
Sprinkle with coconut and chopped nuts.

Cookies, Brownies, and Bars

Delvin looks forward to baking day in hopes of getting his share of the delicious goodies!

AMARANTH BROWNIES

Combine:

1³/₄ cups amaranth flour
¹/₄ cup carob powder
¹/₂ tsp. salt

2 tsp. soda
1 tsp. guar gum
¹/₂ cup chopped nuts

Set aside.

Combine:

1 cup hot water
¹/₃ cup olive oil
2 Tbsp. warmed white grape juice concentrate

Quickly, with as few strokes as possible, combine wet and dry ingredients.
Pour into greased 8 x 12" pan.
Bake at 425° F. for 20 - 25 minutes.
Spread with "Carob Date Icing" (page 114) while still hot.

QUINOA BROWNIES

Beat:

1 cup applesauce
¹/₂ cup olive oil
1 Tbsp. vanilla

1 cup peanut butter
2 eggs or ¹/₄ cup applesauce
³/₄ cup carob powder

Add:

2 cups quinoa flour
2 tsp. baking powder
2 tsp. soda

2 tsp. stevia
¹/₂ tsp. salt
¹/₂ cup chopped nuts

Mix until just moistened.
Spread on greased jellyroll pan.
Bake at 350° F. for 25 - 30 minutes.

BROWNIES

(Pictured on front cover.)
1 cup mashed banana
$^2/_3$ cup olive oil
4 eggs or 2 tsp. guar gum + $^1/_2$ cup water
$^1/_2$ tsp. vanilla
$^1/_2$ cup apple or grape juice or water
3 cups spelt or kamut flour
$^2/_3$ cup carob powder
$^1/_2$ tsp. soda
$^1/_2$ tsp. cream of tartar
1 tsp. stevia

Combine wet ingredients and beat well.
Add flour and carob powder. Beat again.
Add rest of ingredients, beating until just mixed.
Pour into greased jelly roll pan.
Bake at 350° F. for 30 - 35 minutes.

PUMPKIN BARS

(day 1)

Beat:
4 eggs or 2 tsp. guar gum + $^1/_2$ cup water
2 cups mashed pumpkin
$^1/_2$ cup olive oil

Add:
2$^1/_2$ cups amaranth or oat flour
1$^1/_2$ tsp. stevia
2$^1/_2$ tsp. baking powder
1 tsp. soda
1 tsp. cinnamon
$^1/_2$ tsp. nutmeg
$^1/_2$ tsp. salt

Mix until just combined.
Spread out evenly on a greased jelly roll pan.
Bake at 350° F. for 30 - 40 minutes.

ALMOND BUTTER COCONUT BARS

Heat in large saucepan:
1/4 cup olive oil

Add:
1 cup rolled oats or spelt
1 cup nuts, chopped
1/3 cup unsweetened, shredded coconut
1/4 tsp. salt

Toast lightly over medium heat, stirring constantly.

In small mixing bowl, combine:
1 cup almond butter or peanut butter
1 tsp. stevia
1 cup juice or water
1 tsp. vanilla
1 tsp. guar gum
1 small ripe banana

Add to the oats and nut mixture.
Cook for 5 minutes, stirring constantly.
Spread the mixture in greased 8 x 12" pan.
Bake at 325° F. for 25 - 30 minutes.
Cool and cut into bars.

CAROB CHIP BARS
(day 3)

Beat:
4 Tbsp. olive oil
4 eggs or 1 tsp. guar gum + 1/2 cup water
1 Tbsp. vanilla

Add and mix:
2 1/2 cups kamut flour
2 tsp. baking powder
1/2 tsp. salt
1 tsp. stevia

Fold in:
3/4 cup carob chips

Bake in greased 9 x 13" pan at 350° F. for 30 minutes.

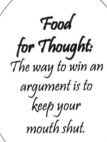

*Food
for Thought:
The way to win an
argument is to
keep your
mouth shut.*

KAMUT (OR) RYE FIG BARS
(day 3)

FILLING:

8 oz. dried figs   2 tsp. vanilla
1 cup water

Stem figs and combine all ingredients in saucepan. Simmer, covered, for 20 minutes. Whiz in blender until smooth.

DOUGH:

3 cups kamut or rye flour   1 cup olive oil
1½ tsp. guar gum   ½ cup cold water + 2 Tbsp.
½ tsp. baking powder

Mix dry ingredients. Add oil and stir until crumbly. Add enough water to make a moist, soft dough. Let set 15 - 20 minutes. Add a little more water if too dry.
Press half of dough into greased 8 x 12" baking pan.
Spread with above filling.
Roll out second half of dough between 2 sheets of waxed paper and place dough on top of filling.
Bake at 400°F. for 30 - 35 minutes.
Cool 10 minutes and cut into 1½" squares.   Yields 3 dozen bars

BANANA CAROB CHIP COOKIES

Beat:
¾ cup olive oil
2 cups mashed bananas, very ripe

Add and mix:

6 cups spelt flour   1 tsp. cinnamon
1 Tbsp. baking powder   1 tsp. nutmeg
2 tsp. soda   ¼ tsp. cloves
1 tsp. cream of tartar   1 tsp. salt
1 tsp. stevia

Stir in:
1 cup carob chips
1 cup chopped nuts

Drop by spoonfuls onto cookie sheet and flatten slightly.
Bake at 350° F. for 12 minutes.   Yields 3 dozen cookies

Spiritual Nugget:
God will give you His best as you give Him your best.

CAROB CHIP COOKIES

3/4 cup water
1 cup applesauce
2 tsp. vanilla
4 1/2 cups spelt flour
2 tsp. soda
1 tsp. baking powder

1/2 tsp. salt
1 tsp. guar gum
2 tsp. cream of tartar
2 tsp. stevia
1 cup chopped nuts
1 1/2 cups carob chips

Beat first 3 ingredients.
Add rest of ingredients and mix until just blended. Do not overmix!
Drop by spoonfuls onto cookie sheet and flatten.
Bake at 375° F. for 12 minutes.

Yields 4 dozen cookies

BARLEY COOKIES

(day 4)

Combine:
1/3 cup olive oil
1 1/2 tsp. vanilla
2 cups barley or spelt flour
1 tsp. stevia
1 tsp. guar gum
1 Tbsp. baking powder
1/2 tsp. salt

Slowly add:
1/2 cup juice, rice milk, nut milk, or water

Drop by spoonfuls onto cookie sheet.
Bake at 350° F. for 12 - 14 minutes.

Yields 12 cookies

PEANUT BUTTER COOKIES
(day 3)

In a saucepan, cook 20 minutes:
3/4 cup water
1/2 cup figs or (1 tsp. guar gum - omit cooking)

Blend until smooth.

In mixer bowl, beat:
1 cup peanut butter
1 1/2 tsp. vanilla
2 eggs or 1 tsp. guar gum + 1/4 cup water
1/2 cup olive oil

Add:
3 cups kamut or spelt flour
1 tsp. soda
1 tsp. baking powder
1 1/2 tsp. stevia

Add fig mixture and mix.
Drop by teaspoonfuls onto baking sheet.
Flatten with a fork in criss-cross style.

Bake at 375° F. for 15 minutes.   Yields 2 1/2 dozen

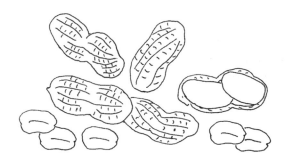

PECAN SANDIES
(day 2)

Beat:
1/2 cup olive oil
1/4 cup apple juice or water
1 Tbsp. vanilla
2 eggs or 1 tsp. guar gum + 1/4 cup water

Add and mix:

2 cups spelt or kamut flour	1/2 tsp. stevia powder
1 Tbsp. baking powder	1/2 tsp. cream of tartar
1 tsp. salt	1 cup finely ground pecans

Fold in:
1/2 cup chopped pecans

Mix all ingredients together until just combined.
Shape dough into cookies.
Place on cookie sheet.
Bake at 375° F. for 17 - 20 minutes.

PUMPKIN WALNUT COOKIES
(day 1)

Beat:
1/4 cup olive oil
1 cup mashed pumpkin
1 tsp. vanilla

Add:

2 1/2 cups amaranth or oat flour	1 tsp. cinnamon
2 tsp. baking powder	1/2 tsp. nutmeg
1 tsp. soda	1/4 tsp. ginger
1/2 tsp. cream of tartar	1 tsp. stevia

Fold in:
1 1/2 cups chopped walnuts, optional

Drop by rounded teaspoonfuls onto cookie sheet.
Bake at 375° F. for 12 minutes.

SHORTBREAD COOKIES
(day 4)

Beat:
2 eggs or 2 tsp. guar gum + $\frac{1}{2}$ cup water
$\frac{1}{2}$ cup olive oil
$\frac{1}{2}$ tsp. vanilla

Add:
2 cups rice flour
4 tsp. baking powder
$\frac{1}{2}$ tsp. cream of tartar
$\frac{1}{4}$ tsp. salt
1 tsp. stevia

Mix on medium speed until just combined.
Drop onto cookie sheet. Flatten.
Bake at 375° F. for 10 - 12 minutes.

When substituting guar gum for eggs it works best to add guar gum with dry ingredients, rather than wet.

Yields 18 cookies

SPICE COOKIES
(day 2)

Beat:
$\frac{1}{2}$ cup olive oil
$\frac{1}{3}$ cup applesauce
2 tsp. maple flavor

Add:
2 cups spelt or kamut flour
$\frac{1}{2}$ tsp. cream of tartar
2 tsp. baking powder
1 tsp. stevia
1 tsp. cinnamon
1 tsp. ginger
$\frac{1}{4}$ tsp. salt
$\frac{1}{2}$ cup chopped nuts

Mix until just combined.
Drop by spoonfuls onto cookie sheet. Flatten.
Bake at 350° F. for 12 - 15 minutes.

Food for Thought:
Take time to laugh, for it is the music of the soul.

Desserts

*Fresh fruit combinations
are a real "hit" with guests.*

APPLE CRISP

(day 2)

A quick, delicious dessert using canned pie filling

2 quarts "Apple Pie Filling" (page 160)
Spelt crumb topping (page 141)

Spread pie filling in 8 x 12" pan.
Spread crumb topping over filling.
Bake at 350° F. for 40 minutes.

APPLE DESSERT

(day 2)

In a mixing bowl, combine:
1³/₄ cups spelt flour
¹/₂ tsp. salt
1 tsp. stevia
¹/₂ cup olive oil

Press into a greased 8 x 12" pan.

Arrange over top of crust:
4 cups shredded, peeled apples

Sprinkle over apples:
2 Tbsp. lemon juice
1 tsp. cinnamon

Bake at 375° F. for 20 minutes.

Meanwhile, combine:
2 Tbsp. applesauce
¹/₃ cup apple juice or water
1 tsp. vanilla
³/₄ cup chopped walnuts or sunflower seeds
1¹/₃ cups flaked coconut, optional

Spread over baked apples and bake 20 minutes longer.
Serve warm or chilled.

Hint:
Pesticides on fruits can be removed by using a mild all-purpose bio-degradable soap. Then rinse in vinegar water and finally rinse with clear water.
It is best to peel waxed fruits and vegetables because the wax is difficult to remove. The wax tends to seal pesti-cides and chemicals into the skin. Locally grown produce is preferable as it is less likely to be treated with chemicals to preserve it.

APPLE DUMPLINGS

(day 2)

2 Tbsp. olive oil
$2^2/_3$ cups spelt flour
2 tsp. baking powder
$^1/_4$ tsp. cream of tartar
$^1/_4$ tsp. salt
$^3/_4$ cup + 2 Tbsp. water

Mix all ingredients together. (Add more flour if sticky.)
Cut 8 medium apples in half. Peel and core.
Divide pastry in 8 equal parts.
Roll each piece out in a circle.
Brush olive oil over pastry.
Sprinkle cinnamon over pastry and over center of apple.
Put 2 halves together and place in center of pastry.
Form pastry around apple, sealing at top of apple.
Place in baking pan.
Brush tops with olive oil.
Prick tops with a fork to allow steam to escape.
Bake uncovered at 375° F. for 50 minutes.

Optional: Fill apple cavities with raisins.

Note: Freeze leftovers for a quick dessert.
Allow to thaw 1 hour.
Bake loosely covered with foil at 375° F. for 40 minutes.

BAKED APPLES

(day 2)

4 sweet fall apples
cinnamon
$^1/_2$ cup apple or white grape juice concentrate, optional

Halve and core apples. Sprinkle inside of each half with part of the concentrate and cinnamon. Put apple halves together. Place in baking pan on the side so juice doesn't run out. Pour remainder of concentrate over apples.
Bake <u>uncovered</u> at 350° F. for 45 minutes or until tender.
Serve warm.

BERRY CRISP

(day 4)

2 quarts blackberries or raspberries
3/4 cup water
1/3 cup cornstarch or arrowroot starch
1 1/2 tsp. stevia
1/2 tsp. cinnamon

In a saucepan bring berries to a boil.
Meanwhile dissolve cornstarch or arrowroot starch in water.
Add stevia and cinnamon.
Pour into boiling berries, stirring until bubbly and thickened. (If using arrowroot, bring just to a boil. Remove from heat and stir in arrowroot.)
Pour into an 8 x 8" baking pan.
Top with Rice Flour Crumb Topping (page 142).
Bake at 350° F. for 35 minutes.

Food for Thought: The heart is happiest when it beats for others.

FROZEN STRAWBERRY DESSERT

CRUST:

1/2 cup olive oil
1 cup spelt flour
1 cup rolled oats or spelt

Press into 8 x 12" pan.
Bake for 12 minutes at 350° F. Cool.

FILLING:

Whip until soft peaks form:
3/4 cup egg whites
2 Tbsp. apple juice concentrate
pinch salt

Set aside.

Beat:
3 cups fresh or frozen strawberries, thawed
1 cup crushed pineapple, undrained
1/2 tsp. stevia

On low speed, fold egg whites into strawberries. Pour over crust.
Freeze. Remove from freezer and refrigerate 1 hour before serving.

FRESH FRUIT COMBINATIONS

Fresh fruit combinations are a big hit with guests.
Be creative and create your own combinations, or try any of
the following:

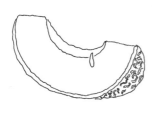

> Watermelon, cantaloupe, and honeydew melon
>
> Cantaloupe, strawberries, and kiwi
>
> Peaches and blueberries
>
> Honeydew melon and blueberries
>
> Apples, grapes, and bananas (dip apples and bananas
> into lemon juice)

Use the most of the first fruit listed in each combination.
Cut into bite size pieces.
Serve in a pretty clear or white glass bowl.

FRUITY TAPIOCA

In 2 cup measuring cup, put:
³/₄ cup tapioca

Cover with warm water to 2 cup mark.
Set aside to soak.

Soak:
3 Tbsp. plain gelatin in:
1 cup "Juicy Juice Fruit Punch"

Bring to a boil:
5 cups "Juicy Juice Fruit Punch"
1 tsp. salt

Drain water off tapioca and stir tapioca into boiling juice. Continue
cooking and stirring until tapioca is clear.
Stir gelatin into boiling tapioca.

Remove from heat and add:
1 tsp. vanilla
12 drops liquid stevia

Cool and add any mixture of fruit; peaches, pears, seedless
grapes, bananas, or berries.

GLORIFIED RICE

3 cups cooked brown rice, cooled
1 ripe banana, mashed
1 cup pineapple
1/4 tsp. stevia
1 tsp. vanilla
1/8 tsp. salt

Stir banana, vanilla, stevia, and salt into pineapple.
Add pineapple to rice and stir. Chill and serve.   4 - 6 servings

MELON MEDLEY
(day 1)
1 large cantaloupe (balls)
1 honeydew melon (balls)
2 cups seedless grapes
2 - 3 bananas, sliced and dipped in orange or lemon juice

Combine chilled fruits and serve.

ORANGE JULIUS
(Pictured on front cover.)

2 cups rice milk
12 oz. orange juice concentrate
1 tsp. vanilla
2 cups crushed ice

Blend all ingredients in blender until smooth.

Allergic to orange juice?
Try grape juice, undiluted (steamer method or concentrate)

Tip:
When buying cantaloupe, smell the vine end of the melon. It should smell sweet like a melon. If that fresh, sweet melon aroma is not there, the melon probably is not good.

ORANGE CREAMSICLES

3 cups rice or soy milk
1$\frac{1}{2}$ cups orange juice concentrate

1 tsp. vanilla
1 tsp. guar gum, optional

Mix in blender. Freeze until slushy and almost frozen. Blend again and pour into popsicle molds or small cups with a popsicle stick inserted. Freeze.

Crave sherbet? Serve in dishes after blending the second time. This tastes a little like sherbet.

Note: This may be too sweet for hypoglycemics.

Variation: Purple grape juice concentrate may be used instead of orange.

PUMPKIN PIE SQUARES

CRUST:
1 cup spelt or oat flour
$\frac{1}{2}$ cup rolled oats or spelt
$\frac{1}{2}$ tsp. stevia
$\frac{1}{2}$ cup olive oil

Combine and press into greased 9 x 13" baking pan. Bake at 350° F. for 20 minutes.

FILLING:

In blender, combine:
3 cups soy or rice milk
2 cups mashed pumpkin
4 eggs
1 tsp. stevia

2 tsp. cinnamon
1 tsp. salt
1 tsp. ginger
$\frac{1}{2}$ tsp. cloves

Sprinkle over top:
$\frac{3}{4}$ cup chopped nuts

Bake at 350° F. for 65 minutes or until a knife inserted in the center comes out clean. Refrigerate.

RASPBERRIES AND DUMPLINGS

Delicious

In a pan, bring to a boil:
1½ cups apple juice
1 pint black raspberries or blackberries

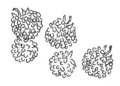

Dumplings:

2 Tbsp. olive oil
1½ tsp. baking powder
¾ tsp. vanilla

1¼ cups rice flour
⅛ tsp. salt
⅓ cup fruit juice or water

Stir together and drop walnut size dumplings in sauce.
Cover and simmer 20 minutes.
Delicious served warm.

RHUBARB CRISP

(day 2)

3 cups chopped rhubarb
4 Tbsp. spelt or rice flour
1 Tbsp. apple juice or water
½ tsp. stevia

Mix above ingredients and place in greased 8 x 12" pan.

Mix:
½ cup olive oil
1½ cups spelt or rice flour
½ tsp. stevia
¼ cup applesauce
¼ cup chopped walnuts

Crumble over rhubarb mixture.
Bake at 375° F. for 40 minutes.

Food for Thought:
Rivers and men become crooked by following the path of least resistance.

RHUBARB CRUNCH
(day 2 use arrowroot starch)

¹/₂ cup olive oil
2 cups spelt flour
¹/₂ cup rolled spelt
2 tsp. cinnamon
¹/₂ tsp. stevia

Mix above ingredients.
Pat half of crumbs into greased 8 x 12" pan.

Spread over crumbs:
5 cups diced rhubarb

Combine in small saucepan:
2 cups apple juice or water
4 Tbsp. cornstarch or arrowroot starch
2 tsp. vanilla
1 tsp. stevia

Bring to a boil, stirring constantly.
Cook 2 - 3 minutes for cornstarch. For arrowroot starch remove
from heat as soon as boiling.
Pour over rhubarb.
Top with remaining crumbs.
Bake at 350° F. for 45 minutes or until rhubarb is tender.

TOFU FRUIT SHAKE

6 oz. soft tofu, drained
1 cup unsweetened pineapple juice
1 banana, fresh or frozen
1 cup raspberries, strawberries, or blackberries

In blender, blend all ingredients until smooth.   Serves 2

Pies

Danae can help by sprinkling crumbs over top of the sour cherry pie.

APPLE PIE

(day 2)

4 cups pared and sliced apples
1¼ cups apple juice or water
3 Tbsp. clear jel
1 tsp. cinnamon
dash nutmeg
1 tsp. liquid stevia

Stir all ingredients together in saucepan.
Bring to a boil and cook 2 minutes. Pour into pie crust (page 141).
Put crumb topping on top (page 141).

Bake at 350° F. for 35 - 40 minutes.

CRANBERRY APPLE PIE

(day 2)

In blender, chop:
1¼ cups apple juice or water
1 cup cranberries
1 tsp. stevia
3 Tbsp. spelt flour

Pour into saucepan.

Add:
4 cups peeled, sliced apples
1 tsp. cinnamon
dash nutmeg
pinch salt

Stir together. Bring to a boil and cook 2 minutes.
Remove from heat.

Add:
2 tsp. maple flavor
½ cup chopped nuts

Pour into unbaked spelt pie shell.
Sprinkle crumb topping over (page 141).
Bake at 350° F. for 35 minutes.

Food for Thought:
To err is human, but if the eraser wears out before the pencil, we are overdoing it.

BLUEBERRY PIE

(day 3)

4 cups blueberries
$1/2$ cup water
2 Tbsp. tapioca starch or cornstarch
1 tsp. stevia
pinch salt

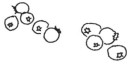

Line cooled prebaked pie shell with 2 cups of the blueberries.
To make sauce, cook remaining blueberries in $1/4$ cup of the water.
Stir tapioca starch, stevia, and salt into the remaining cold water,
and stir into boiling berries.
Cook 2 minutes, stirring constantly.
Cool and pour over berries in pie shell.
Chill.

SOUR CHERRY PIE

(day 2)

$3^1/2$ cups sour cherries, with juice
$1/2$ cup apple juice or water
4 Tbsp. arrowroot or cornstarch
1 tsp. stevia
1 tsp. cinnamon

Hint:
For pre-
baked pie
shell, bake at
375° F. for 15
minutes.

In saucepan, bring cherries to a boil.
Meanwhile, dissolve arrowroot or cornstarch in juice or water.
Pour into boiling cherries.
Stir until boiling. (Do not boil arrowroot.)
Remove from heat.
Add stevia and cinnamon.
Pour into pie shell and sprinkle crumb topping over top (page 141).
Bake at 350° F. for 35 minutes.

PEACH PIE

(day 4)

In kettle, combine:
4 cups fresh peeled peaches, sliced
2 Tbsp. water
3 Tbsp. minute tapioca
$1/4$ tsp. stevia

Bring to a boil and cook 1 minute while stirring constantly.
Pour into crust.
Sprinkle with $1/4$ tsp. cinnamon over pie.
Spread crumbs over top (page 142).
Bake for 10 minutes at 425° F.
Lower oven temperature to 350 ° F. and bake 25 minutes longer.

Note: For **Pear Pie** - Substitute pears for peaches.

*Food for
Thought:*
*Blunt remarks,
like dull knives,
often inflict the
most severe
wounds.*

PUMPKIN PIE

(day 1)
1 unbaked pie shell

In blender, process:
$1/4$ cup white grape juice concentrate
1 tsp. stevia
1 tsp. guar gum
1 tsp. cinnamon
$1/4$ tsp. nutmeg
$1/4$ tsp. salt
2 cups cooked pumpkin, mashed
$1 1/2$ cups soy, cashew, or rice milk

Blend until just combined.
Pour into pie shell.
Bake at 425° F. for 15 minutes.
Reduce to 350° F. and bake 40 minutes longer.
Pie will set up when cool.

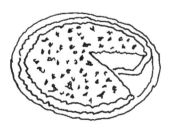

COCONUT PIE CRUST
(day 4)
A little crumbly, but delicious!

$^1/_2$ cup olive oil
1 cup brown rice flour
$^1/_2$ cup coconut
$^1/_2$ tsp. cinnamon
$^1/_2$ cup chopped walnuts

Mix together and press into pie pan.
Bake at 375° F. for 10 minutes or fill and bake according to pie directions.

Yummy for blueberry or peach pie!

OATMEAL PIE CRUST
(day 1)

1 cup oat or spelt flour
$^2/_3$ cup rolled oats or rolled spelt
$^1/_4$ tsp. salt
$^1/_3$ cup olive oil

Combine dry ingredients.
Drizzle oil over while mixing.
Add a little water (1 - 2 Tbsp.) if needed to form a soft ball.
Pat dough into 9" pie pan.
Fill and bake according to pie directions or bake shell at 400° F. for 10 minutes.

SPELT PIE CRUST
(day 2 or 3)

3 Tbsp. olive oil
2²/₃ cups spelt or kamut flour
2 tsp. baking powder
¹/₄ tsp. salt
²/₃ cup water

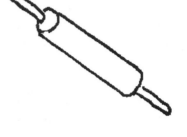

Mix oil and dry ingredients.
Add water.
Mix quickly until dough forms a ball.
Divide dough in two.
Roll out on a floured countertop.
Fold in half and place in pie pan.
Unfold and trim around edge of pan and flute edges.

Makes 2 single crusts

SPELT CRUMB TOPPING   (FOR PIES)
(day 2)

¹/₃ cup olive oil
1¹/₂ cups spelt flour
¹/₂ cup chopped nuts

Mix together.
Sprinkle over 2 pies and bake.
Half of topping can be refrigerated for up to 2 weeks.

Food for Thought:
Whenever we are
in the wrong place,
our "right" place
is empty.

BRAN CRUMB TOPPING (FOR PIES)
(day 1 or 4)

1/2 cup olive oil
1 1/2 cups oat, rice, or spelt flour
1/2 cup chopped nuts
1/2 cup oat or rice bran

Mix together with a fork.
Sprinkle over 2 pies and bake.
Half of topping can be refrigerated for up to 2 weeks.

RICE FLOUR CRUMB TOPPING (FOR PIES)
(day 4)

2 cups rice or millet flour
1/4 tsp. salt
1/3 cup olive oil
3 Tbsp. cold water

Mix flour and salt.
With a fork stir in olive oil.
Add cold water.
Sprinkle over 2 pies and bake.
Half of topping can be refrigerated for up to 2 weeks.

100%
Whole
Grain

Miscellaneous

The Vita-Mix is quite valuable in making one's own foods like "Almond Butter".

ALMOND BUTTER
(day 2)

2 cups raw almonds
$^1/_4$ tsp. salt

$^1/_2$ cup olive oil
$^1/_4$ tsp. stevia

Preheat oven to 350° F. Spread almonds in shallow pan.
Drizzle $^1/_4$ cup of the oil over almonds. Sprinkle with salt.
Bake 15 minutes or until toasted.
Place nuts, stevia, and the rest of the oil in Vita-Mix or blender.
Process at medium speed, using tamper, until smooth and creamy.
Store covered in refrigerator or freezer. Stir to blend in oil or pour off
before using.

Variations:
Raw cashews or peanuts may be used in place of raw almonds,
using only half as much oil.
Raw Almond Butter: Use same amount of each ingredient, leaving
almonds raw.

FIG BUTTER
(day 3)

Cook, covered, for 20 minutes:
2 rounded cups dried figs
2 cups water

Remove from heat.

Add:
1 tsp. vanilla

Whiz in blender until smooth.
Cool and spread thinly on kamut bread or bread of your choice.
Sprinkle with chopped peanuts.

Yields 8 - 10 sandwiches

Raw peanuts contain enzyme inhibitors that make it difficult for your body to digest protein. Roast at 350° F. for 25 minutes. Stir and roast an additional 25 minutes.

CHEESE (DAIRY FREE)
Grate over pizza, bean burritos, or casseroles, or cut cheese sticks for snacks.

Place in blender and soak 5 minutes:
1 cup boiling water
6 Tbsp. gelatin

Blend just enough to mix.

Add and blend until creamy:
1 cup almonds or sunflower seeds
1 small garlic clove or $1/8$ tsp. garlic powder, optional
1 Tbsp. diced onion

Add:
$1/2$ cup chopped carrot
$1/4$ cup nutritional yeast flakes
1 Tbsp. lemon juice concentrate
$1/2$ tsp. paprika
1 tsp. salt

Blend until smooth, scraping sides.
Pour into greased loaf pan.
Refrigerate.

Note: Agar-agar flakes can be used in place of gelatin:
(This cheese tends to be softer, and it may work better to slice than shred it.)

In small kettle, soak 5 minutes:
1 cup water
4 Tbsp. agar agar-flakes

Bring to a boil and simmer 5 minutes, stirring occasionally.
Pour into blender. Proceed with recipe.

Note: Extra cheese may be grated and frozen.

Allergic to almonds? Substitute almonds with 1 cup well cooked northern or any white beans.

SOY YOGURT

Heat to 112° F.:
1 quart soy milk

Add:
$1/2$ tsp. vanilla, optional

Stir in:
1 Tbsp. (10 grams) dry yogurt culture

Pour into warm jar.
Cover, leaving a small opening to avoid liquid floating on top.
Let set at room temperature, covered with a towel to keep heat in,
for 14 - 18 hours or until set, or in 105° F. oven for 4 - 8 hours.
Refrigerate immediately without disturbing.

Save $1/4$ cup to make next batch in place of dry yogurt culture.

Yields 1 quart

Tip:
Vegetables
can be quickly
diced
or chopped in
blender on
"pulse" or in
Vita-Mix.

VEGETABLE BROTH
(day 1)

7 cups water
2 large carrots, diced
1 medium onion, mince
1 clove garlic, minced
1 green pepper, chopped
1 large tomato, chopped
$1/2$ tsp. oregano
$1/4$ tsp. dill
$1/4$ tsp. basil
salt to taste

Bring to a boil. Cover and simmer 1 hour.
Strain or puree in blender.
Use in place of meat broth.

Hint: It saves time to make broth in larger quantities and freeze for
later use.

HOMEMADE VINEGAR

Use fresh cider made from good quality, clean apples. Poor quality cider will sometimes spoil instead of fermenting into vinegar.

Fill clean jugs with cider, leaving several inches of head room for cider to "work".

Cut circles from cheesecloth to fit over top of jugs and secure with rubber bands or string. Caps may be loosely set on top.

Set in a warm place and allow to ferment. Set the jugs on trays in case they foam over.

It will usually form its own "mother" - a thick gelatinous mass floating on top. When it does that, you will know your vinegar making is a success.

When it is completely done working and it tastes like vinegar, strain and store in clean jugs. The vinegar may be heated after it is strained to stop the aging process.

SUMMER SUET (FOR THE BIRDS)

(Use year-round, but it is especially good for in summer because it holds up in warm weather.)

Melt over low heat:
1 cup lard or rendered suet
1 cup crunchy peanut butter

Stir in:
$1/3$ cup sugar

Add and mix well:
1 cup whole wheat flour
2 cups oatmeal
2 cups cornmeal
bird seed, optional

Pour into pans and cool.
Cut into squares and place into suet feeders.

Hint: We like to put it in mesh bags and hang it so the starlings can't get at it.

Snacks

Darla pops up a batch of popcorn –
a favorite snack of the Steiner family.

GUACAMOLE

1 Tbsp. olive oil
2 tsp. lemon juice
2 fully ripened avocados
1 medium tomato
1 medium onion, chopped (about 1/2 cup)
1/4 tsp. sage
1/4 tsp. basil
1/4 tsp. salt

Tip:
Avocados are ripe
when they turn dark and
are slightly softened.
Halve, peel, and pit
to use.

Place all ingredients in blender.
Blend on medium speed until just barely blended.
It should be a little chunky.
Store in refrigerator.
Serve at room temperature with chips, celery, or peppers.
Best if used within 2 days.

GARLIC BARLEY CRACKERS

2 cups barley flour
1 Tbsp. onion, finely minced
1 Tbsp. parsley flakes
1/2 tsp. salt
1/2 tsp. cream of tartar
1 tsp. soda
1/8 tsp. garlic powder
1/4 tsp. stevia
1/2 cup olive oil
1/2 cup grape juice

Mix all ingredients except juice. Add juice, making a stiff dough.
Roll out thin on cookie sheet.
Cut into squares and prick each cracker with fork.
Bake at 400° F. for 12 - 15 minutes.

BARLEY CRACKERS
(day 4)

Mix:

2 cups barley flour

1 tsp. soda

$^1/_2$ tsp. cream of tartar

$^1/_4$ cup olive oil

$^1/_2$ tsp. salt

$^1/_4$ tsp. stevia

$^1/_4$ tsp. cumin

Add and mix until combined:

$^1/_2$ cup prune juice or water

Roll out thin on cookie sheet.
Cut in squares.
Bake at 375° F. for 15 minutes. Cool.

Can be stored at room temperature up to 4 days.

Tip:
Try olive oil
for popping
popcorn.

RYE CRACKERS
(day 1)

Mix:

2 cups rye flour

$^1/_2$ tsp. salt

$^1/_2$ tsp. garlic powder

$^1/_4$ cup oat bran

1 tsp. baking soda

$^1/_2$ tsp. cream of tartar

1 Tbsp. onion, minced fine

$^1/_3$ cup olive oil

Add and mix to make a stiff dough:

$^1/_2$ cup grape juice

Pat onto greased cookie sheet $^1/_8$" thick.
Cut into squares with pizza cutter.
Bake at 400° F. for 15 minutes.
Can be stored at room temperature for up to 4 days.

SPELT THINS

(day 2)

2½ cups spelt flour
1 cup rolled spelt or oats
1 tsp. baking powder
¼ tsp. stevia

½ tsp. salt
¾ cup olive oil
½ cup water

Mix dry ingredients. Add oil and water and combine.
Add a little water if crumbly.
Roll out thin on cookie sheet.
Sprinkle with salt if desired. Cut in squares.

Bake at 350° F. for 15 - 20 minutes.

KAMUT CRACKERS

(day 3)

2¾ cups kamut flour
¼ tsp. celery seed
¼ tsp. thyme
½ tsp. guar gum

1 tsp. baking powder
½ tsp. salt
½ cup olive oil
¾ cup water

Combine dry ingredients. Mix in oil and water.
Roll out thin on cookie sheet.
Cut in squares.
Bake at 350° F. for 15 - 20 minutes.

PARTY MIX

A delicious snack you can serve to guests!

½ cup olive oil
1 tsp. paprika
¼ tsp. celery seed
¼ tsp. onion powder
½ tsp. garlic salt
10 oz. Cheerios
8 oz. pretzels
1 lb. salted, roasted peanuts

Mix oil and seasonings. Drizzle over last three ingredients. Toss.
Spread on baking pan and toast at 250° F. for 2 hours, stirring every
20 minutes.
Note: If you are allergic to peanuts try Deluxe Mixed Nuts.

> **Tip:**
> We use
> "Arrowhead
> Mills" Natures
> 'O Cheerios; and
> "VitaSpelt" spelt
> pretzels, which
> contain no
> sweeteners.

SOFT PRETZELS - (SOURDOUGH)
(day 2)

In non-metal bowl measure, using a non-metal spoon:
1 cup sourdough starter
1½ cups warm water
3½ cups spelt flour

Allow to set at room temperature overnight or 6 hours.

Into sponge mixture, add:
½ cup apple juice concentrate, warm
1 Tbsp. vinegar, optional
1 Tbsp. olive oil
1½ tsp. salt

Beat until just mixed.

Add:
3½ - 4 cups spelt flour

Flour should be room temperature.
Cover and allow to rise 2 hours.
Punch down.
Divide dough into 24 pieces.
Roll each one into a long rope.
Make pretzel shapes.
Use water to glue 2 parts together.
Place on greased baking pan.
Additional salt can be sprinkled over pretzels.
Allow to rise again for 1½ hours.
Bake at 400° F. for 20 minutes.

Canning and Freezing

It is rewarding to be able to can, freeze, and store the bountiful harvests.

CANNING AND FREEZING
Without Sugar

FRUIT (PEACHES, PEARS, CHERRIES, PLUMS, ETC.)

Peel and slice or chunk peaches or pears.
Place in jars.
Fill with any of the following syrups.
Process 20 minutes in hot water bath.

SYRUP (FOR CANNING ANY FRUIT)

• 3 Tbsp. liquid stevia per quart of water. White grape juice may also be used for a better tasting, sweeter fruit.

• 1 Tbsp. powdered stevia per quart of water. Bring to a boil and strain through cheesecloth or a thin cloth.

• Try using apple juice.

• Use white grape juice, diluted, 2 parts juice to 1 part water.

• If fruit is not very sweet, do not dilute juice.

• Peaches and pears are also good with pineapple juice.

• If you slice fruit into jars instead of halves, it tends to be sweeter because it is less diluted. (More fruit goes in.)

(continued)

Hint: Pesticides on fruits can be removed by using a mild all-purpose bio-degradable soap. Then rinse in vinegar water and finally rinse with clear water.

It is best to peel waxed fruits and vegetables because the wax is difficult to remove. The wax tends to seal pesticides and chemicals into the skin. Locally grown produce is preferable as it is less likely to be treated with chemicals to preserve it.

CANNING AND FREEZING
(CONTINUED)

APPLESAUCE

Tip:
Apples with red peels should be frozen for a pretty pink sauce. Canning turns it brown.

Tips for a sweeter sauce:

Use sweet fall apples that are fully ripened such as: Yellow Delicious, Cortland, or Grimes. Yellow Delicious and Grimes are delicious mixed together. We can one kind and freeze the other to keep them separate, then combine to serve to guests.

Leave peels on, cores in, and cut into 8 sections.

Cut apples into salty water until ready to cook. It sweetens them and keeps them from turning brown.

Experiment with the amount of water needed to cook apples. Use no more than necessary. Medium to thick sauce is sweeter. Strain.

Liquid stevia may be used to sweeten applesauce. (Stevia containing alcohol should be added while sauce is still hot.) Try a little and taste; however, be careful that you don't use so much that you can taste the stevia!

Note: Save the pulp that comes out of the Victorio strainer. Run it through one more time and use the thick sauce for apple butter.

APPLE CIDER

When cider is in season, can your own. It is sweeter and more concentrated. Use it in place of milk in cereal or in place of apple juice in baking.

Boil cider 10 minutes. Warm jars in 200° F. oven. Heat rings and lids. Pour cider in warm jars and seal <u>or</u> pour cold cider in jars, seal, and cold pack 20 minutes.

FREEZING BANANAS

Freeze for blender shakes or for eating plain. Cut in half lengthwise. Spread out on cookie sheet and place in freezer until frozen. Store in plastic bags in freezer.

FREEZING BERRIES

Raspberries, blackberries, and blueberries should not be washed unless they are sprayed or are dirty. Freeze in airtight bags or freezer boxes.

Tip: When purchasing peaches, look for locally grown or tree ripened peaches. Avoid hydro-cooled peaches.

FREEZING CHERRIES

SWEET CHERRIES: Wash and freeze with seeds in. Remove from freezer 1 hour before serving. They are delicious partly frozen.

SOUR CHERRIES: Wash and remove seeds, or purchase fresh pitted cherries. Check ingredients. Some contain sugar! Freeze.

FREEZING GRAPES

Seedless grapes are delicious frozen.
Wash and remove stems. Spread out on cookie sheet and place in freezer until frozen. Store in plastic bags in freezer.

FREEZING STRAWBERRIES

Strawberries taste sweeter if chopped rather than crushed or mashed.

Freeze some whole for desserts and frozen blender desserts.

APPLE PIE FILLING I (MAKES 7 QUARTS)

Soak:
1 cup quick cooking tapioca in:
1¹/₂ cups cider

Bring to a boil:
7 cups cider

Add tapioca and continue cooking, stirring constantly, until thickened and bubbly. Cook an additional 2 minutes.

Remove from heat and stir in:
3 Tbsp. liquid stevia
2 tsp. cinnamon
1 tsp. salt
¹/₄ tsp. nutmeg

Stir into:
35 medium size, sweet apples, sliced and peeled
Pack tightly into jars almost to neck.
Coldpack 15 minutes at a rolling boil.

Tip:
We like Yellow Delicious for a nice sweet apple to be used in apple pie fillings.

APPLE PIE FILLING II (MAKES 8 QUARTS)
Enjoy a fresh apple pie!
Bring to a boil:
7¹/₂ cups cider

Dissolve:
1¹/₂ cups clear jel in:
2 cups cider

Gradually pour into boiling cider while stirring.
Boil 1 minute. Remove from heat.

Add:
3 Tbsp. liquid stevia
1 Tbsp. cinnamon
3 Tbsp. lemon juice

Stir into:
40 medium, sweet apples, sliced and peeled
Pack tightly into quart jars, filling almost to neck.
Coldpack 15 minutes at a rolling boil.

BLACKBERRY PIE FILLING

Bring to a boil:
28 cups blackberries
1 cup white grape juice or water

In another kettle bring to a boil:
5 cups white grape or apple juice or water

Combine and stir into boiling juice:
2 cups minute tapioca
3 Tbsp. stevia
1 Tbsp. salt
2 Tbsp. cinnamon

Boil and stir constantly for 2 - 3 minutes. Stir into berries.
Place into 7 quart jars. Seal and coldpack 20 minutes.

CHERRY PIE FILLING

Bring to a boil:
26 cups pitted sour cherries in juice

Mix together:
1 cup cornstarch
3 Tbsp. stevia
$1/8$ tsp. salt
1 cup white grape or apple juice or water

Stir into boiling cherries. Continue stirring and allow to boil 2 minutes.

Add:
2 Tbsp. cinnamon

Pack into 7 quart jars.
Seal and coldpack 20 minutes.

Note: When measuring cherries, pack them down.

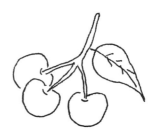

FRUIT SLUSH

3½ cups white grape juice or water
4 Tbsp. liquid stevia
5 quarts peaches, peeled and sliced
3 lb. red seedless grapes
8 bananas, sliced

Stir well and put into freezer containers.
Freeze.

To serve, remove from freezer and refrigerate 2 - 4 hours.
Serve slushy.   Yields 8 quarts

STRAWBERRY JAM
(This jam uses Pomona's Universal pectin - a 100% citrus pectin.)

Bring to a boil:
6 cups mashed strawberries
1 Tbsp. calcium water

Meanwhile, mix together:
1 Tbsp. pectin powder
1 tsp. stevia

Add:
½ cup white grape juice concentrate

Mix well and stir into boiling fruit.
Stir vigorously 1 - 2 minutes to dissolve pectin.
Return to boiling and remove from heat.
Fill freezer containers.
Allow to cool. Freeze.

APPLE BUTTER

Mix together in roaster:
16 cups thick applesauce
2 Tbsp. cinnamon
$^1/_2$ tsp. cloves
1 tsp. stevia

Add:
4 cups cider or apple juice concentrate

Bake uncovered at 350° F. for 4 hours or until desired consistency, stirring occasionally.
Pour into heated jars.
Seal with hot lids.
Turn upside down until cool.

Note: To save on baking time, save the pulp that comes out of the Victorio strainer.
Put pulp through again after sauce has all been put through.
Use this thick sauce for part or all of your apple butter.

Tip:
When open kettle canning anything except juices, we turn jars upside down after tightening lids. They are surer to seal. Turn upright when cooled.

PEAR BUTTER

12 cups pear sauce
1 Tbsp. cinnamon
1 Tbsp. stevia

Put in roaster and bake at 350° F. uncovered for 3 hours, or until desired thickness, stirring occasionally.
Put into heated jars and seal with hot lids and rings.
Turn upside down until cool.

Note: Raw pears may be pared and pureed in blender. Then follow recipe.

CUCUMBER RELISH

Finely grind or process in blender with a little water:
20 large cucumbers
4 large onions
4 sweet peppers

Combine and soak for 1 hour in $1/4$ cup salt and water to cover.

Bring to a boil in a large pan:
$1/2$ cup frozen white grape juice conc.   2 cups white vinegar
1 tsp. mustard seed   1 Tbsp. celery seed
1 tsp. turmeric   2 tsp. stevia
2 tsp. ground mustard

Drain vegetables in colander. Add vegetables to syrup and heat.
Simmer 10 minutes.
Fill warm jars and seal.   Yields 10 - 12 pints

Hint:
To warm jars, place in 200° F. oven along with jar rings. Cover lids with water in kettle on top of stove and bring to a boil.

DILL PICKLES

Cucumbers, enough to fill 7 quart or 14 pint jars
Slice cucumbers $1/4$" thick or quarter lengthwise.
Fill jars half full.

Add:
1 small clove garlic
1 sprig dill

Fill to top of jars with cucumbers.
Put grape leaf on top, pushing down around edge of jar.

Brine:
4 cups white or apple cider vinegar
1 cup salt
8 cups water
$1/2$ tsp. stevia, optional

Bring to a boil and fill jars to the top. Seal tight.
Coldpack 10 minutes.

KETCHUP

1 - 2 hot peppers	1 onion, sliced
1 clove garlic	4 quarts tomato chunks
2 red bell peppers	1 stalk celery, chopped

Cook until soft. Pour or ladle clear juice off top. Strain in Victorio strainer.
Strain in pillowcase 1/2 hour, discarding clear juice.

In blender, mix:

3/4 cup vinegar	1 tsp. cloves
1 tsp. cinnamon	1 tsp. dry mustard
1 Tbsp. salt	1 tsp. stevia

3 - 6 Tbsp. clear jel or arrowroot starch
(1/2 tsp. red pepper if hot peppers are not available)

In a large kettle bring strained tomatoes to a boil.
Stir in blended ingredients.
Cook, stirring constantly, for 2 minutes, or longer if a thicker ketch-up is desired. (Do not cook arrowroot.)
Pour into hot jars and seal.   Yields 4 - 6 pints

Quick cook tip: After cutting tomato chunks to cook for juice, etc., go in with both hands and squeeze juice out of tomatoes. Saves lots of cooking time.

PIZZA SAUCE

4 quarts tomato juice	1 tsp. black pepper
1 onion, chopped fine	1 tsp. oregano
1 tsp. parsley flakes	2 Tbsp. salt
1 garlic clove or 1 tsp. garlic powder	1 Tbsp. Italian seasoning
1/4 cup olive oil	1/2 tsp. stevia

1 - 2 hot peppers or 1/2 tsp. cayenne pepper

Process all of the ingredients in the blender except juice.

Add to blender and process again:
1 cup clear jel or cornstarch

Stir into boiling juice.
Bring to a boil. If not thick enough, thicken with more clear jel or cornstarch, softened in a little cold water. It will be thicker when cold. Put in jars and coldpack 25 - 30 minutes.

Hint: When harvesting small amounts of tomatoes, wash and cut them up ready to cook. Put them in plastic bags and freeze. When ready to make ketchup or pizza sauce, thaw overnight. Drain juice off and cook pulp.

LENTIL SALSA

4 tomatoes, peeled
1 stalk celery, chopped
1 medium onion, chopped
2 cloves garlic, minced
1 sweet pepper, chopped
4 jalapeno peppers, minced (remove seeds if you like it mild)

2 cups cooked lentils
$1/2$ tsp. stevia
1 Tbsp. salt
1 Tbsp. olive oil

Process small amounts of vegetables and lentils in blender on pulse. Pour into large kettle. Bring to a boil. Boil for 5 minutes, stirring constantly, or until desired thickness. Put into jars and seal. Coldpack 25 minutes.

SALSA

Mix and bring to a boil:
10 cups peeled, chopped tomatoes
2 cups seeded green peppers, chopped
4 jalapeno peppers, chopped, or $1/2$ - 1 Tbsp. crushed red pepper
2 cups chopped onions
1 clove garlic, finely chopped
$1^1/2$ tsp. salt
2 tsp. oregano
$1/2$ tsp. cumin
1 tsp. chili powder
1 tsp. paprika
1 tsp. stevia

Add and cook down $1^1/2$ - 2 hours:
$1/4$ cup vinegar or lemon juice
                    or
Dissolve and stir into salsa and cook 5 - 10 minutes:
3 Tbsp. cornstarch or clear jel in:
$1/4$ cup vinegar or lemon juice

Fill jars and seal.
Coldpack 20 minutes.

Tip:
Wear rubber gloves to cut hot peppers or hold on to stem and cut on a cutting board, being careful not to touch cut pepper or seeds.

To coldpack:
Place filled jars in canner. Cover with warm water. Cover and bring to a rolling boil. Begin timing. Reduce heat as needed, but keep boiling. Remove jars as soon as time is up.

PICKLED BEETS

25 small beets
1¹/₂ cups vinegar
2¹/₂ cups water
1 Tbsp. salt
1 Tbsp. cinnamon
1 tsp. allspice
1 tsp. stevia

Select young beets. Cook until tender.
Dip in cold water and peel off skins. Put in jars.
If larger beets are used, cut in chunks.
Make syrup with above ingredients. Boil 5 minutes. Pour over beets.
Seal and coldpack 10 minutes.   Yields 5 pints

TOMATO JUICE COCKTAIL

8 quarts ripe tomatoes, quartered but not peeled
2 medium onions, peeled and chopped
4 stalks celery with most of leaves on, cut in short pieces
2 small to medium carrots with leaves, chopped
1 hot pepper - adjust according to hotness desired
2 sweet peppers, cut in pieces
2 cloves garlic   1 bouquet parsley
1 Tbsp. salt   2 red beet leaves
¹/₂ tsp. oregano, optional

> **Tip:**
> Whenever you make tomato juice, do tomato juice cocktail! It makes delicious soups and is also wonderful for drinking!

   Place tomatoes in a large pot, mashing them as you go to form
juice. Add remaining ingredients (see note below). Simmer over
low heat till vegetables are tender. Put through food mill or Victorio
strainer. Put hot into jars and coldpack 15 minutes.

Note: (If using a food mill it works best to puree the raw vegetables
in the blender. Pour them over the tomatoes in the pot and simmer
until tomatoes are soft. With the Victorio strainer, the vegetables
just need to be chopped.)
   Vary the vegetables to your liking. The secret to this delicious
juice is that no water is added. It is all pure juice.

CANNED BEANS

1½ cups (scant) dry beans in quart jar
Fill to neck with water.
1 tsp. salt, optional

Pressure can for 90 minutes at 11 lbs. pressure,
or coldpack for 3 hours.

Tip:
Try canning green beans without water. Just pack the beans into the jar, tighten the lid, and process like usual. Makes them taste more like fresh, because there is no water to absorb the flavor.

CANNING MEAT

Tightly pack ground beef, chunk beef, chicken, or turkey into pint or quart jars.
Do not add water.
Add ½ - 1 tsp. salt to each jar.
Seal and process in pressure cooker 90 minutes at 11 lbs. pressure, or coldpack for 3 hours.

CHICKEN WITH BROTH:
Cover chicken with water and cook until tender. Debone, chop, and fill jars with chicken and broth. Process according to instructions above.

CANNING POTATOES
(Need a way to use those little potatoes?)
Scrub small potatoes (golf ball size and smaller).
Put in wide-mouth quart jars.
Add 1 tsp. salt to each jar if desired and fill with water.
Seal and pressure can at 11 lb. pressure for 45 minutes.

To serve: Rinse potatoes and shred for hash browns.
Fry in olive oil, turning only once to prevent them from getting mushy.

Tip:
For potatoes and green beans canned with water, rinse 2 times when opening jar for better taste.

CANNING TOMATO CHUNKS

Cut stem ends out of tomatoes.
Scald tomatoes by dipping in boiling water for 1 minute.
Slip skins off.
Pack into quart jars.

Optional, add:
1 tsp. salt, dash of pepper, and ¼ tsp. ginger to each quart jar.

Seal and coldpack 45 minutes.

Hint: Delicious baked over meatballs or meat loaf, or add to soup.

FREEZING ASPARAGUS

To harvest, break spears off at ground level when they are 6 - 8 inches long (before spear head opens).
Snap tender end of spear off, discarding bottom woody part.
Wash thoroughly and cut into 1 inch pieces.
Blanch just until asparagus color deepens, 1 - 2 minutes.
Cool and freeze.

FREEZING CORN
(Tastes almost like fresh when done this way.)

Silk corn and cut off cob.
Cover bottom of kettle or skillet with water. Add corn and blanch just until corn turns a deeper yellow.
Pour into another container and cool quickly by placing in ice water.
Package and freeze.

FREEZING ONIONS

Chop onions that won't keep for the winter.
Place 2 rounded Tbsp. on pieces of saran and wrap individually.
Put the packets into a larger sealed container or jar to keep odors from mingling with other foods. Freeze. Real handy when in a hurry!

FREEZING PEPPERS

Green peppers can be finely chopped and frozen.
Place 1 or 2 Tbsp. on pieces of saran and wrap individually.
Put the packets into a larger container to keep pepper odor from mingling with other foods. Freeze.
Just take out a packet to use in recipes calling for peppers.

FREEZING ZUCCHINI

No need to peel. Shred, package, and freeze.

CANNING CARROTS

Fill quart jars with bite size chunks. Fill with water and ½ tsp. salt. Pressure can for 30 minutes at 11 lb. pressure.

Carrots are slow coming up?
When sowing carrots, cover lightly with sawdust to retain moisture for better germination and for weed control. Water occasionally with a light sprinkling of water.

FREEZING CARROTS

Chop carrots (small amounts at a time) in blender or finely dice. Blanch, then freeze in small packages for quick additions to casseroles and soups.

STORING CARROTS IN GROUND

Carrots may be planted at various intervals through the summer. (We make our last planting after digging potatoes. The ground is fine and soft from digging.) Carrots like loose, sandy soil. Try planting them in hills, adding sand if you have clay soil. When carrots are 2 inches tall, thin to 2 - 3 inches apart, using the tiny carrots.

Leave carrots in the ground over winter. After the first ground freeze, cover the carrot rows with leaves or straw to keep the ground from freezing.

Dig as you are ready to use or whenever you have a warmer day. Dig enough for several weeks. They keep in the refrigerator for 3 - 4 weeks.

To keep carrots from rotting over top, uncover them after freezing weather is over.

Carrots sown in summer should be dug before they start growing in the spring. Carrots sown in early fall will continue growing in the spring. Dig as needed.

APPENDIX

-- *Stocking the Pantry*--

Most of these items can be found at Food Co-ops, Health Food Stores, Bulk Food Stores, or check in the "<u>Resources</u>" section for suppliers.

<u>**Agar Powder:**</u> A vegetarian gelatin made from a marine algae. Mostly an indigestable complex carbohydrate that adds bulk to the diet. Use instead of gelatin.

<u>**Carob Powder:**</u> Carob is a substitute for chocolate, and is high in calcium and trace minerals. There are some individuals that have an intolerance for carob, causing fatigue.

<u>**Gelatin:**</u> is used to avoid artificial sweeteners and dyes. Use fruit juice in place of water for flavor.

<u>**Grains:**</u> The various grains are available from food co-ops, health food stores, or you may be able to obtain them from a local farmer at a considerable savings.

<u>**Guar Gum:**</u> is 80% soluable dietary fiber. Add to low gluten breads or use in place of eggs as a binder in baked goods.

~Stocking the Pantry (Cont.)~

Olive oil: We recommend and use only olive oil. If you don't like olive oil, use canola for salad dressing. Gradually add and increase amount of olive oil as you learn to appreciate the taste. Olive oil contains oleic acid, which is a monounsaturated fat. Oleic acid is an antioxidant, and also tends to lower blood pressure, and help regulate blood sugar levels. Some people need to rotate brands occasionally to avoid intolerance.

Buy <u>"Extra Virgin, Cold Pressed"</u> olive oil. It is pressed from the olive fruit. Olive oil labeled "pomace" or "contains pomace" is made by extracting oil (usually chemically) from the pits and leftover pulp after the first 2 pressings. It may be inexpensive, but it is not worth buying, as the flavor is not as good, and the health benefits have been mostly removed.

Some brands we use are: **Bertolli, Golden Barrel, Marconi, Omaggio, and Spectrum.**

Salt: <u>Celtic Sea Salt</u> is a naturally moist salt containing a balanced mixture of essential minerals. Because of the moisture, it works best added to liquid and stirred to dissolve. (We like it for everything except baking.) Some people required to be on a salt free diet find they are able to use Celtic salt in moderation. For more information, or to order, call 1-800-867-7258 or www.celtic-seasalt.com.

<u>Real Salt:</u> natural mineral sea salt with no chemicals added. It has not been heated or cooked in processing. (We use this salt for baking.)

<u>Bio Salt:</u> a fine textured salt found in health food stores. Some persons required to be on a salt free diet also find that they can use small amounts of this salt.

Stevia: (more information in the **"Sugar Free Diet"** section, page 191)

~Stocking the Pantry (Cont.)~

Thickeners:

Arrowroot Starch or Flour: nutritious and is easier to digest than wheat. The root of this plant is dried and ground into powder. Use half as much as flour called for in recipes. Dissolve in a small amount of water before adding to boiling liquid. Bring to a boil, then turn burner off. Do not cook after adding arrowroot or it may lose its thickening power. It also does not hold its thickening power when reheated. Just add more arrowroot starch.

Clear jel: waxy modified corn.

Cornstarch: produces the most pleasing results, and is the best thickener if you are not allergic to corn.

Poi (Taro): Easily digestable.

Potato starch or flour: It may be necessary to process in blender to eliminate lumps.

Tapioca starch or powder: is derived from the manioc plant root.

Tofu: is a fermented soybean product, and therefore is more easily digested than soybeans. Be careful if you are allergic to soy. Tofu can be found in refrigeration sections of supermarkets, co-ops, or health food stores.

Yogurt culture: Dry powdered culture is available in the refrigeration section of health food stores.

Xanthan Gum: very similar to Guar Gum, but is higher priced. Persons with candida should be careful because it is derived from a fungi. Also, if you have a corn allergy make sure there is no corn in it.

-Helping Yourself-

Try keeping a food diary of all the foods you eat for 2 to 3 weeks.

Be sure to note any symptoms you develop. (You may need to list ingredients in some foods.) You will soon see patterns. Eliminate any foods you suspect for at least 3 to 4 weeks.

First you may want to eliminate such high allergy foods as <u>wheat</u>, <u>dairy</u>, <u>eggs</u>, <u>corn</u>, <u>refined sugar</u>, and <u>soy</u>. Also, any foods you crave should be discontinued. Be sure to eliminate any suspect foods from your diet.

You may suffer with some withdrawal symptoms for a few days, such as headaches, nervousness, or irritability.

After the body is cleared of the allergens, gradually reintroduce the foods, one at a time. After a food is reintroduced, wait at least 4 days to try another one.

Some foods may need to be retested several times. You may experience delayed reaction to another food you reintroduced earlier.

Some foods are better tolerated if cooked rather than raw.

-Keeping a Food Diary-

Write down everything you take into your mouth, including vitamins, medications, gum, etc.

Keep meals simple, large portions of a few foods, rather than a variety. That way it is easier to detect any problem food.

Be specific. List ingredients, including spices and seasonings.

Write down all of your symptoms, how severe, and how long after eating the symptoms appeared. Some possible symptoms may be: rapid heartbeat, hives, sores in mouth, hyperactivity, irritability, insomnia, headache, depression, sinus drainage, asthma, shortness of breath, etc.

Look for patterns at the end of the week. If you react each time you eat a certain food, suspect it as an "allergy" or "intolerance" food.

To completely cleanse your body of the allergy food, totally eliminate it for 3 months. Then you may try it again, **but only once every 4 days!**

Rotate <u>all</u> foods every 2 - 4 days, or you may develop a sensitivity to an often used food. **NOTE:** Foods you were sensitive to, do not use oftener than every 4 days. You may need to limit any foods you were oversensitive to, to one time a day every 4 days.

Make extra foods and freeze the extras. Mark container according to what day it is - day 1, day 2, day 3, or day 4.

-Whole Grain Varieties-

Most of these grains can be found at Food Co-ops, Health Food Stores, Bulk Food Stores, or check in the "Resources" section for suppliers.

Whenever possible, buy your grains from a supplier that has a fast turnover and keeps them under refrigeration. After you buy your grains, store them in the refrigerator or freezer to maintain freshness.

You might try getting your grains from a local farmer for better prices. If you can get them soon after harvest and store them in a cool place, you will be assured of fresh quality.

Barley: Barley is one of the cereal grasses, and has a bran similar to rice bran. The bran contains all the vitamins, minerals, and oils. Without refrigeration the bran will turn rancid. Be sure to buy your barley from a supplier that keeps it refrigerated. Pearled barley has part of the bran removed. It is white, and is almost pure starch. We do not recommend it, as most of the nutrition has been removed along with the bran. Barley contains a water soluble fiber, forming bulk which helps to relieve constipation. Barley has a low gluten content and will not rise well as a yeast bread.

Kamut: Kamut is an ancient high protein grain - approximately 17% protein, and is a relative of durum wheat. It has never been hybridized. Studies have shown that around 70% of people that are sensitive to wheat are able to use kamut. Kamut flour can be used in any recipe without altering the amount of any of the ingredients, except that slightly more liquid may be needed. Although it is considered a high gluten flour, it has less gluten than wheat. While that is no problem in most baked goods, yeast breads will have slightly less volume.

-Whole Grain Varieties (Continued)-

Oats: a starchy grain, and contains 67.5% carbohydrates and 16.1% protein. It is a good source of vit. B1, calcium, fiber, and unsaturated fat. When baking, the finished product tends to be a little heavier and wetter. <u>Oat Bran is high in fiber.</u> Try using it in baking and cooking. It tends to help stabilize blood sugar imbalances.

Rye: is high in carbohydrates and contains 5.9% protein. It is often mixed with other grains in bread making.

Spelt: Spelt is an ancient variety of wheat, but does not cause the problems wheat does. It is a great alternative for those suffering from wheat allergies, and is easily digested. It is higher in protein, amino acids, and most minerals than wheat.

Wheat: Modern wheat has been hybridized for higher yield, easier growing and harvesting, and higher gluten content for high-rising fluffy yeast breads. Wheat is considered one of the highest allergy causing foods, possibly due to all the hybridizing. We do <u>not</u> use wheat in our recipes. Sprouting wheat may be considered by persons with wheat allergy, as the culprit is often the gluten. Sprouting will get the vitamins and minerals into a form usable by many wheat allergic people.
    Try **Sprouted Grain** breads such as **Ezekiel 4:9.** Most wheat allergy problems are caused by the gluten in the wheat, and it is destroyed in the sprouting process.

Gluten-free grains: Check the **"Gluten Free Diet"** section for information on each of the following grains: **Amaranth, Buckwheat, Corn, Millet, Quinoa, Rice,** and **Soy.**

--Allergies--

Skin rash, abdominal cramps, asthma, eczema, sores, tingling, itching of lips or mouth, hives, phlegm, headaches, ear infections, hearing problems, fatigue, muscle pains, hyperactivity, poor concentration, irritability, diarrhea, constipation, itchy, watery, or puffy eyes, dark circles under the eyes, frequent nosebleeds, bloating, and cramps are often indications of one or more food allergies.

Allergy sensitivity is often inherited. If one parent has allergy problems, the child has a 50% chance of also developing allergies. If both parents have allergy problems, the child has at least a 75% chance of developing allergies.

Food allergies may be brought on one's self by over-indulgence. Favorite foods should be eaten in moderation.

<u>Dairy products</u>, <u>eggs</u>, <u>seafoods</u>, <u>wheat</u>, <u>soy</u>, <u>peanuts</u>, <u>nuts</u>, <u>corn</u>, <u>citrus</u>, and <u>berries</u> are all high allergy foods.

Many people who have environmental allergies find that they also have food allergies. When these foods are avoided, the environmental allergies nearly or totally disappear.

(Continued)

--Allergies (Continued)--

Many people who believe they are hypoglycemic, or have candida or yeast infection, have allergies. Therefore avoiding allergy foods helps to eliminate the symptoms.

Some food reactions are caused by intolerances, rather than allergies, and may occur because of insufficient enzymes to digest the food, such as the enzyme lactase to digest milk (lactose intolerance). Some reactions are caused by preservatives, such as sulfites, metabi-sulfites, benzoate, butylated hydroxyanizole-tolene (BHA and BHT). Dyes (red dye #3,4,5: yellow dye #5 and 6; blue dye #1 and 2) and tartrazine azodyes, flavor enhancers, monosodium glutamate (MSG), and natural salicylates.

For information about delayed reaction food allergies and the Ig G ELISA blood test, call IMMUNO LABORATORIES at 1-800-231-9197.

--Read Those Labels!--

Make a habit to always check labels!

Allergies and Sensitivities:

Corn: Since corn in some form or other is found in so many foods, it is difficult to totally avoid. Watch out for baking powder, dextrin, cornstarch, mazola oil, sorbitol, glucose, fructose, dextrose, invert sugar, corn syrup, corn sugar, grits, hominy, maize, popcorn, corn chips, pudding, distilled white vinegar, xanthum gum, MSG, and HVP. Avoid anything with the word, "corn". Following are some foods that likely contain corn: starch, food starch, or modified food starch, iodized table salt, pill binders, vegetable "anything" such as vegetable oil, broth, protein, shortening, caramel flavoring, or major brands of pure vanilla. **More information in "Corn Free Diet" section (page 184).**

Egg: Look for and avoid such names as: albumin, yolk, vitellin, ovovitellin, livetin, globulin, ovomucin, and ovomucoid. **More egg allergy information in "Egg Free Diet" section (page 185).**

Gluten: There are some grains that are high in gluten. Some are low in gluten. And there are those that contain no gluten. **To learn more about gluten free grains check "Gluten Free Diet" section (page 186-188).**

Milk derivatives appear in non-dairy products. Watch for such names as: casein, caseinate, sodium caseinate, whey, lactose, lactoglobulin, and curds. **More on milk allergy in "Milk Free Diet" section (page 189).**

-- Read Those Labels! (Cont.) --

Monosodium glutamate (MSG): Symptoms most often are headaches, asthma, or depression after eating food containing monosodium glutamate. It is added to foods to enhance the flavor of many packaged and processed foods. Many restaurants add MSG to their foods. It may be derived from soy, wheat, or seaweed. MSG is not always listed in the ingredients of foods. "HVP" or "natural flavorings" in foods may contain up to 20% MSG, and not need to be listed. One example is tuna.

Nut: Symptoms to watch for are eczema and gastric problems. Avoid peanut and other nut oils that you may be sensitive to.

Soy: appears in many foods. Be on the lookout for such things as: TVP (texturized vegetable protein), HVP (hydrolyzed vegetable protein, lecithin, and soybean oil. **More on soy allergy in section "Soy Free Diet" (page 190).**

Sugar: Watch for: sucrose, glucose, lactose, dextrose, levulose, maltose, karo syrup, corn syrup, corn sweetener, invert sugar, maple sugar, cane sugar, cane syrup, syrup, raw sugar, sorbitol, polysorbate, molasses, honey, and fructose. **More on sugar allergy in "Sugar Free Diet" section (page 191-193).**

Wheat: may show up in rice or rye breads, as well as in many other foods. Watch for such names as: gluten, graham flour, monosodium glutamate (MSG), hydrolyzed vegetable protein (HVP), durum flour, semolina, and bulgur.
More on wheat allergy in section "Wheat Free Diet" (page 194).

--Corn Free Diet--

Some symptoms of corn allergy are: <u>eczema,</u> <u>hives, abdominal pain,</u> <u>diarrhea,</u> and <u>respiratory problems</u>. Also <u>muscle pain, fatigue,</u> <u>headache,</u> <u>hyperactivity,</u> and <u>poor concentration</u>.

Some substitutes you can try for cornstarch and clear jel are: <u>potato, arrowroot, taro, or tapioca starch.</u>

In baking, <u>millet flour</u> makes a very good substitute.

Avoid: See corn section in **"Read Those Labels"** (page 182). Corn is a most versatile food, and is used in a wide variety of processed goods. It is almost impossible to stay completely away from corn without making everything yourself from "scratch".

Corn is a highly manipulated plant. We do well to leave genetically engineered foods out of our diet.

--Egg Free Diet--

Some symptoms of egg allergy are: gastric distress (as listed under "milk allergy") and eczema.

Flax seed egg substitute:
> **Grind:**
> 1/4 cup flax seed
>
> **Bring to a boil, stirring constantly:**
> 1 1/2 cups water
> ground flax seed
>
> Boil 3 minutes.
> Cool and refrigerate in covered container.
> 2 Tbsp. equals 1 egg.

The following substitutes equal one egg:

1 small to medium banana, mashed

2 Tbsp. thick applesauce

2 Tbsp. prune butter

1/2 tsp. guar gum + 2 Tbsp. water

1/4 cup tofu

1 Tbsp. arrowroot or cornstarch + 3 Tbsp. water

1 Tbsp. plain gelatin + 2 Tbsp. warm water

Use immediately.

Avoid: Bought baked goods, puddings, cream pies, soft candy, and noodles.

--Gluten Free Diet--

Some symptoms of gluten intolerance are: weight loss, diarrhea, bone pain, mild weakness, and gastric problems.

Low-gluten and no gluten flours do not work well for yeast breads. They work best for quick breads, such as muffins, biscuits, pancakes, waffles, cakes, cookies, and bars. See gluten-free bread (page 21).

All the grains can be used for breakfast cereals. Try cracking them in the blender for tasty hot cereals. They also work well in grain dishes for the main meal.

The following grains contain gluten:

Low-gluten: barley, oats, rye, triticale, teff, and soft wheat
High gluten: hard wheat, kamut, and spelt

Avoid: all products containing wheat, oats, rye, barley, or their derivatives. This is difficult because many processed foods have many hidden sources of gluten found in their ingredients. Rarely does a person react to all gluten containing foods. Experiment until you know which ones you react to, but use them in moderation!

See following pages for gluten free grains.

(continued)

--Gluten Free Diet (Cont.)--

USE THE FOLLOWING FOR A GLUTEN FREE DIET:

Amaranth: Amaranth is a grain-like plant used by the Native Americans. It is high in <u>lysine</u> which makes it a more complete protein on its own. It is high in essential fatty acids-14%, and has a <u>protein content of 15 - 18%</u>. it is also high in vitamin E and other vitamins and minerals.

Buckwheat: Buckwheat is not a true grain, although it is usually considered a grain. It is best to buy "toasted" buckwheat, because untoasted buckwheat sometimes has a moldy smell or taste. Persons with candida or mold allergies may react to it. We recommend <u>Buckwheat, kasha, toasted.</u>

Corn: Corn is a rich source of <u>fats</u>, <u>proteins</u>, and <u>carbohydrates</u>. Be sure you do not react to it, as it is considered a high allergy food.

Millet: Millet is the seed of an annual grass. It is high in amino acids, protein, iron, magnesium, phosphorus, and potassium, as well as lysine which makes it a more complete protein. This grain is very alkaline, helping an acidic system to become more alkaline. Few people are allergic to it.

(continued)

--Gluten Free Diet (Cont.)--

<u>Quinoa</u>: (Pronounced "keen-wah") Quinoa is a grain-like plant used by the Incas, and is about <u>16.2% protein</u>. It is also high in <u>lysine</u>, making it a more complete (usable) protein on its own. It is also high in <u>essential fatty acids-13.5%, calcium, iron</u>, and <u>B vitamins</u>. Rinse before cooking.

<u>Rice</u>: Rice is a nutritious grain and contains almost 80% carbohydrates and 8% protein. It has a rough outer hull which is removed. The kernel within is surrounded by a series of brownish skins called bran coats. <u>Use only brown rice.</u> White rice is polished and has the vitamins, minerals, amino acids, and fiber removed. Buy your brown rice from a supplier that keeps it refrigerated, and keep it refrigerated after you buy it or else the bran which contains all the oils and amino acids will get rancid. Try <u>wild rice</u> for variety. We like to mix brown and wild rice. Wild rice contains 14% protein. Rice crops are heavily sprayed. Consider using organic rice, especially if you are sensitive to chemicals.

<u>Soy</u>: Be sure you do not have a soy allergy, since soy is considered a high allergy food. Tofu is made from soybeans and is more easily digested than soybeans. It can be found in the refrigeration department of the supermarket, food co-op, or health food store. Use it as a substitute for eggs or cheese, or chop in pieces and fry to add to casseroles in place of meat.

--Milk Free Diet--

The #1 suspect for allergies is dairy products.

Some symptoms include: chronic earaches, A.D.D., colds, phlegm, asthma, eczema, headaches, stomach pains, bloating, gas, cramps, diarrhea, and constipation.

Colic in nursing babies can often be eliminated by the mother eliminating dairy products or other allergy foods from her diet. If the mother does not use dairy products during pregnancy, the baby is not nearly so likely to have milk allergies.

Substitutes for milk include: Soy milk, either liquid or powder (watch out though for possible soy allergy), nut milks, rice milk, fruit juice, or just plain water.

Goat milk can be tolerated by some people with milk allergies. Its composition is closer to that of mother's milk, and is easier to digest than cow's milk.

If you have a lactose deficiency, you may be able to eat yogurt, as it contains its own lactose. Make your own, or be sure it contains live culture.

Kosher products labeled pareve or parve do not contain milk.

Beware of: non-dairy creamer, non-dairy dessert topping listing casein (a milk derived sugar), tuna listing hydrolyzed vegetable protein (often contains whey), cheeses, butter, whipping cream, sauces, and gravies.

--Soy Free Diet--

Some symptoms of soy allergy are: <u>hives</u>, <u>gastric distress</u>, <u>depression</u>, <u>hyperactivity</u>, <u>facial swelling</u>, and <u>shortness of breath</u>.

Some of the symptoms in infants include <u>vomiting and diarrhea</u>, <u>skin problems</u>, <u>asthma</u>, and <u>inflamed mucous membranes</u>.

Substitutes: <u>olive oil</u> for soy oil, <u>rice milk</u> for soy milk, and <u>chicken or turkey broth</u> for soy sauce.

Beware of: <u>breads</u>, <u>cake</u>, <u>cereals</u>, <u>ice cream</u>, <u>lecithin</u>, <u>emulcifiers</u>, <u>margarine</u>, <u>salad dressing</u>, <u>salty snacks</u>, <u>soups</u>, <u>tofu</u>, <u>tempeh</u>, <u>miso</u>, <u>natto</u>, <u>tamari</u>, <u>teriyaki</u>, <u>Chinese foods</u>, <u>TVP</u>, <u>HVP</u>, <u>MSG</u>, <u>Worcestershire sauce</u>, <u>soy sauce</u>, <u>processed meats</u>, <u>sausages</u>, and <u>anything with the name "soy" in it</u>.

--Sugar Free Diet--

Some symptoms of sugar intolerance are: <u>cramps</u>, <u>bloating</u>, <u>canker sores</u>, <u>hyperactive</u>, <u>headaches</u>, <u>dry, itchy eyes</u>, <u>depression</u>, <u>low energy</u>, and <u>weak spells</u>.

A good substitute is: <u>stevia</u> *(Stevia Rebaudiana)*. Stevia is a plant in the daisy family, grows naturally in South America, and can be used as an herbal sweetener.

Stevia is very concentrated, taking only a pinch or a teaspoon in recipes. It is 30 - 300 times sweeter than sugar, depending on the type. It contains no calories and helps balance blood glucose, rather than elevate insulin levels. Stevia is safe for those who have candidiasis as it does not feed yeasts in the intestinal tract. Do some experimenting on your own to obtain the end product you like. Too much may give a sweet off-taste that you don't appreciate.

The FDA has approved stevia as a dietary supplement only. Therefore you will not find the word sweetener on the label. Research shows that it is a very safe substitute for sugar or artificial sweeteners which have side affects and health hazards.

It is available in various forms. <u>Dried leaves</u> are excellent for adding to your tea leaves when brewing tea. <u>Green stevia powder</u> is what we use in baking. It is not as sweet as the white stevia. We feel it is the preferred form for anyone with hypoglycemia or diabetes.

<u>White stevia extract</u> or <u>Stevia Blend</u> is bleached and has other ingredients added. Check the label. It tastes good, but often contains maltodextrin.

--Sugar Free Diet Continued--

Liquid stevia comes in 2 forms. The green form is closest to nature. The clear form is made from white stevia extract, and as such often contains maltodextrin.

We use green liquid for syrups for canning and some desserts where fine green leaves would be noticeable.

In our recipes, we use green powdered stevia unless the recipe calls for "liquid stevia".

Liquid stevia is available without alcohol. If using stevia with alcohol, it is preferable to add to boiling ingredients to evaporate the alcohol.

Stevia can be found in your food co-op or health food store, or about anywhere that herbs are sold.

Stevia conversion chart

Sugar	Powdered stevia	Liquid stevia
1 cup	1 tsp.	1 tsp.
1 Tbsp.	$^1/_8$ tsp.	6 drops
1 tsp.	pinch	2 drops

Some people may be able to use barley malt or fruit juice concentrates.

Barley Malt	Powdered stevia	Liquid stevia
$^1/_4$ cup	1 tsp.	1 tsp.

--Sugar Free Diet Continued--

BEWARE!

Check the "Sugar" section in **"Read Those Labels!"** for a list of various sugars to watch out for (page 183).

BEWARE OF ARTIFICIAL SWEETENERS!

Following is a list of artificial sweeteners to steer clear of as much as possible:

Aspartame (Nutra sweet) or (Equal) found in beverages, sugar free Jello, and instant pudding.

Acesulfame K found in desserts, candy, chewing gum, beverages, and Sweet One.

Cyclamates

Saccharin found in soft drinks, chewing gum, several tabletop sweeteners including Sweet 'N' Low, Sweet 10, Sugar Twin, and Sweet Mate.

Sucralose found in desserts, beverages, and tabletop sweeteners.

--_Wheat Free Diet_--

The #2 suspect for allergies is wheat products.

Some symptoms include: sinus problems, eczema, itching, rashes, swelling of face, hands, or feet, hay fever, asthma, gastric distress, constipation, diarrhea, and heart irregularities.

Substitutes for wheat include: barley, oat, rice, quinoa, kamut, rye, millet, and spelt flour; also potato, tapioca, sago, and arrowroot starch.

Avoid: breaded meats, malt products, HVP (hydrolyzed vegetable protein), MSG (monosodium glutamate), and commercially prepared pastas, baked goods, desserts, sauces, and gravies.

Also included are graham, durum, wheat germ, wheat bran, farina, and semolina.

Yeast and Mold Free Diet

Symptoms: Some symptoms of yeast and mold allergies are headaches, gastric problems, joint pain, muscle soreness, yeast infection, and candida.

Avoid: cheese, and any aged foods, yeast, vinegar and foods containing vinegar (salad dressing, catsup, and prepared mustard), mushrooms (fungi), sugar, breads, brewer's yeast, and citric acid. Overripe fruit, leftovers, cantaloupe, and peanuts often have molds on them. Be sure to eat leftovers within 2 days, or better yet, freeze for later use.

Substitutes:

For yeast breads: salt free - yeast free breads found in food co-ops and health food stores, tortillas, and rice cakes (Quaker can be found in grocery stores, and various varieties in co-ops and health food stores).

For vinegar: use lemon juice and distilled white vinegar (made from corn).

For soy sauce: substitute with meat broth and add salt.

For peanut butter: try other nut butters such as almond or cashew, or make your own (page 145).

Look for **other special diet substitutes** at your food co-op or health food store.

Salt Free or Low Salt Diet

TIPS FOR "SALT FREE" COOKING:

Using waterless cookware and cooking as nearly waterless as possible leaves the flavor in the food.

Cook until just tender-crisp. Mushy food tastes flat.

Can your own meats and vegetables without salt. Most commercially canned foods are high in salt or sodium.

Make your own homemade noodles without salt *(See recipe)*.

Use broth from your canned meats to cook pastas, rice, etc.

Adding lots of celery, onion, peppers, or garlic to your food, also tomato juice cocktail *(see recipe),* makes it more tasty.

Barbecue meats plain or brush with salt free butter and/or vinegar.

Try pineapple juice on chicken; or lemon, orange, or pineapple juice on broiled fish.

For tastier foods try hot spices like Cajun; or try Mrs. Dash.

Check labels: Some spices and "salt substitutes" have salt or sodium hiding in them.

Some foods with very high salt content: balogna, ham, wieners, sausage, bacon, cheese, and commercially canned soups.

TIPS FOR "LOW SALT" COOKING:

All the above tips apply to "low salt" cooking also.

Salt vegetables after they are cooked. They will need less. Mushy overcooked foods require more salt.

If using salted canned food items, rinse them off with water before preparing. (I put foods like tuna in a strainer and run water over it.)

Avoid instant hot cereals, and most cold cereals.

Omit or cut in half the amount of salt called for in a recipe.

Try Bio Salt or Real Salt (found in health food stores), or Celtic Salt from The Grain & Salt Society. See "**Resources**".

--~Resources~--

AMSTUTZ PANTRY   330-857-8159
15893 Baumgartner Road
Dalton, OH 44618

They ship. Call or write for a price list.
Brown rice, Barley, Dried beans, Lentils, Unsweetened carob chips, Carob powder, Raw nuts and seeds, Unsweetened pure peanut butter, Fruit juice sweetened jam, Sugar free apple butter, Pomona's Universal Pectin, Powdered barley malt, Stevia extract (white), Stevia Herb (green powder), Real salt, Whole grain flours, Whole grain pastas

ENER-G FOODS   800-331-5222
P. O. Box 84487
Seattle, WA 98124

They carry a selection of alternate grains, mixes, etc., and also egg replacer.

FOOD FOR LIFE   www.foodforlife.com

Bread: Ezekiel 4:9 - (100% flourless sprouted grain) and much more.

HEALTH SOURCES   937-666-6107
P.O. Box 263
Middleburg, OH 43336

Stevia: leaves, powder, or liquid

KITCHEN SPECIALTIES AND GRANARY 419-542-6275
09264 Fountain Street Rd.
P.O. Box 100
Mark Center, Ohio 43536

Juicers, grain mills, sprouters, meat grinders, pasta machines, dehydrators, water distillers; also beans, grains, pasta, flour, and more.

PURITY FOODS   517-351-9231   Fax: 517-351-9391
2871 W. Jolly Rd.
Okemos, MI 48864
www. purityfoods.com

VitaSpelt pasta, grains, flour, and pretzels.
Pancake, muffin, and bread mixes.
Organically grown beans, grains, seeds, dried fruit, nuts, and more.

SMUCKERS

Sugar-free peanut butter, Simply Fruit 100% fruit jam, R.W. Knudsen pure unsweetened fruit juices.
Available in their retail store at Orrville, Ohio; in your local grocery; or call 1-800-742-6729 to order.

Resources, continued

SMITH'S BULK FOOD 330-857-1132
5413 S. Mount Eaton Rd.
Dalton, Ohio 44618

They ship. Call or write for price list.

Alternate flours: whole wheat, spelt, rice, rye - white and dark, soy, buckwheat, oat, and yellow cornmeal.

Raw: nuts, pumpkin seeds, and sunflower seeds.

Pasta: wheat free corn macaroni and spaghetti; and spelt macaroni and spaghetti; brown rice rotini and spaghetti.

Grains: pearled barley, flax seeds, millet, brown rice, and rye berries.

Legumes: lentils, blackeye peas, and black, pinto, great northern, and garbanzo beans.

Sugar free: unflavored gelatin; vanilla, pure peanut butter (just peanuts).

Misc: carob powder, unsweetened carob chips, lecithin granules, arrowroot, potato, and tapioca starch, stevia, guar gum, and Pomona's Universal Pectin.

Resources, continued

NATURE'S FOOD MARKET (No mail orders)
4860 E. Main Street, Berlin, Ohio 44610

Rice milk and soy milk
Carob chips sweetened with barley malt, unsweetened, or dairy free
Sugar free wieners and bologna; ketchup and mayonaise; Ezekiel
bread; corn flakes, crispy brown rice cereal, and many more cereals; Stevia
Beans, grains, and seeds in bulk
Unsulphured dried fruits and nuts
Sprouting seeds, carob powder, guar gum, arrowroot starch, "Bio" and
"Real" salt, and much more.

THE GRAIN AND SALT SOCIETY   **1-800-867-7258**
273 Fairway Drive   **www.celtic-seasalt.com**
Ashville, NC 28805

Celtic Salt, grains, legumes, pasta, seasonings, herbs, oils, butters,
bath and beauty aids, and more.

VITA-MIX   **1-800-848-2649**

WAL-MART SUPER CENTER

"Star Kist" Gourmet Choice Tuna
Cold pressed extra virgin olive oil
Juicy Juice Fruit Punch
Unsweetened frozen fruit juice concentrates
Rice Dream rice drink

WALNUT ACRES   800-433-3998
Penns Creek, PA 17862

Whole grains and flours, seeds and nuts, beans, dried fruits, etc.

INDEX

BREAKFASTS AND BEVERAGES

BREADS

MAIN DISHES

MEATS

SOUPS AND SANDWICHES

SANDWICHES

VEGETABLES

SALADS AND SALAD DRESSINGS

APPLE VIEW PUBLICATIONS
4495 CUTTER ROAD
APPLE CREEK OH 44606

Date:_____

Ship to:Name_____
                        (Please print)

   Street_____

   City_____State_____Zip_____

Please send me:

____copies of **WOW! This Is Allergy Free Cookbook** $10.95 each_____

____copies of **WOW! This Is Sugar Free Cookbook** $10.95 each_____
          (Making the transition from sugar and refined foods)

____copies of **WOW! This Is Low Cholestrol & Sugar Free Cookbook** $10.95 each_____
          (Stevia sweetener and tips on lowering cholestrol the natural way)

Shipping and handling for first book $2.50 _____
Canadian Orders add additional $4.50 (U.S. Funds only) $4.50 _____
Shipping for each additional book to same address   .75 _____
                                            Total $ _____

Orders will be shipped parcel post, book rate
(or)
Add $1.00 extra for UPS

Make checks payable to:
APPLE VIEW PUBLICATIONS

Dealers and distributors, write for more information.

207

APPLE VIEW PUBLICATIONS
4495 CUTTER ROAD
APPLE CREEK OH 44606

Date:_____

Ship to:Name_____
(Please print)

Street_____

City_____State_____Zip_____

Please send me:

_____copies of **WOW! This Is Allergy Free Cookbook** $10.95 each_____

_____copies of **WOW! This Is Sugar Free Cookbook** $10.95 each_____
(Making the transition from sugar and refined foods)

_____copies of **WOW! This Is Low Cholestrol & Sugar Free Cookbook** $10.95 each_____
(Stevia sweetener and tips on lowering cholestrol the natural way)

Shipping and handling for first book $2.50 _____
Canadian Orders add additional $4.50 (U.S. Funds only) $4.50 _____
Shipping for each additional book to same address   .75 _____
Total $ _____

Orders will be shipped parcel post, book rate
(or)
Add $1.00 extra for UPS

Make checks payable to:
APPLE VIEW PUBLICATIONS

Dealers and distributors, write for more information.

Consignment:
· 2 Richard Jolly
· 1st Tifton Love
    Affair
- reticello micalmo ⎫ Tadashi
  - rusty orange   Torii
UPS store
they wrap + ship
· Credit union acct open locally
    for child support

· small stuff consign'nt stuff

4 or 5 larger pieces ⎫
    we'll store ←

⌐···⎤ uv light
       UV glue

160 amp black lamp
    10"

Clean surface
add uv glue
then black light
cure 10-20 sec

(Suzanne Gregg ?)

Maria + Christopher